CW00953522

Memories of Peterborough

Memories of Peterborough

Part of the
Memories
series

The Publishers would like to thank the following companies for supporting the production of this book

Main Sponsor

Perkins Engines Company Limited

APV Baker

Axiom Housing Association Limited

RG Carter Peterborough

British Sugar plc

Nene Housing Society

Sharman Quinney

Stephenson Smart & Company

Thomas & Green

Queensgate Shopping Centre

First published in Great Britain by True North Books Limited
Units 3 - 5 Heathfield Industrial Park
Elland West Yorkshire
HX5 9AE
Tel. 01422 377977

ISBN 1 900463 98 9

Text, design and origination by True North Books Limited
Printed and bound by The Amadeus Press Limited

Memories are made of this

Memories. We all have them; some good, some bad, but our memories of the city we grew up in are usually tucked away in a very special place in our minds. The best are usually connected with our childhood and youth, when we longed to be grown up and paid no attention to adults who told us to enjoy being young, as these were the best years of our lives. We look back now and realise that they were right.

So many memories - perhaps of the war and rationing, perhaps of parades, celebrations and Royal visits. And so many changes; one-way traffic systems and pedestrianisation. New trends in shopping that led to the very first self-serve stores being opened.

Through the bad times and the good, however, Peterborough not only survived but prospered. We have only to look at the city as it is today, with its finest buildings in their full glory now complemented by up-to-the-minute facilities, to see what progress has been realised and what achievements have been made over the last 50 years. Peterborough has a history to be proud of - but more importantly, a great future to look forward to, into the new millennium and beyond.

Contents

Around the city centre

Broadway seems an appropriate centre for entertainment, and this shot, probably taken in the late 1940s, includes not only the Embassy but on the left, the Broadway Cinema, and in the distance, the Empire Theatre, where Harry Hanson's Court Players were in residence until 1958. The theatre closed in November 1959 and demolition began in 1960.

The Broadway - Peterborough's first purpose-built cinema - was opened in 1910 as the Broadway Electric Theatre. Extensive renovations in 1912 gave it a seating capacity of 1,000 and the new name Broadway Kinema which by the 1920s had been shortened to The Broadway. Under the Rank umbrella it became the Gaumont in 1959 but later went eyes down to Bingo, as so many cinemas did during the 50s and 60s. It was demolished in 1987. Many famous feet trod the boards at the Embassy and there was something to suit every taste, offering such diverse performers as Vera Lynn and George Formby as well as ballet and the Royal Philharmonic. The Embassy was built for both live shows and cinema, but in 1955 the appeal of Cinemascope won the day and cinema took over. Live theatre would appear to have been slowly ousted by the silver screen, but the Key Theatre, built in the early 1970s, was of course to change all that....

A glance at the 1930s

WHAT'S ON?

In this heyday of the cinema, horrified audiences were left gasping at the sight of Fay Wray in the clutches of the giant ape in the film 'King Kong', released in 1933. Very different but just as gripping was the gutsy 1939 American Civil War romance 'Gone with the Wind'. Gable's parting words, 'Frankly, my dear, I don't give a damn' went down in history.

GETTING AROUND

At the beginning of the decade many believed that the airship was the transport of the future. The R101 airship, however, loaded with thousands of cubic metres of hydrogen, crashed in France on its maiden flight in 1930. Forty-eight passengers and crew lost their lives. In 1937 the Hindenburg burst into flames - the entire disaster caught on camera and described by a distraught reporter. The days of the airship were numbered.

SPORTING CHANCE

The black American Jesse Owens won a brilliant four world records in the 1936 Olympic Games in Berlin, thumbing the nose to Adolph Hitler's dreams of Aryan superiority. In a petty display Hitler walked out of the stadium and 'took his bat home'; later he refused to have his photograph taken with the victorious Owens.

Why was it that ice cream always tasted better when we were young? Readers will surely remember being taken to Stapleton's Dairies to buy ice cream, and for some a visit to the famed establishment was a regular weekly treat. Old as well as young enjoy their ices, however, so perhaps the gentleman wearing the cap and the mini-skirted young girl are both about to call in for a '99'! Others in search of refreshment,

however, might have preferred a quick pint of their favourite brew at the Rose and Crown next door. It seems strange to remember that two-way traffic was allowed in Bridge Street at the time of this 1960s photograph; today, of course, the street is a pedestrianised area.

Road works were ahead of drivers, however, on this particular day, and a diversion sign warns motorists that they will have to take an alternative route to wherever they want to go. So what's new? This 'Alice through the Looking Glass' approach to motoring (head off in the opposite direction to your destination) has become familiar to drivers around the city, who find themselves facing holes in the road and sets of temporary traffic lights with tedious regularity.

CHEMIST
GFL 495
BOVIS
WALTON
MFA 960

Left: This gleaming saloon car will undoubtedly have left a few passers-by green with envy, but from this angle we cannot help noticing that its driver has nevertheless parked it rather carelessly, with one wheel on the pavement.
The advert outside the chemist on the left will jog a few memories; how long is it since we saw Ilford films for sale? From time to time, products disappear from our shops without warning, and it is often months or even years later that we realise that they have gone. Fry's Five Boys chocolate, Omo washing powder, Carter's Little Liver Pills, Fennings fever powders, Charles Atlas body-building courses ('You too can have a body like mine!'), Smiths crisps with a little blue bag of salt.... We could go on and on. And remember the Saracen's Head on the right? In its early years this rather nice old pub was blessed with an ornamental portico - lit by two lamps - around the entrance. The first Saracen's Head, which stood in the Market Place as long ago as the 1400s, was along with the Black Swan among the oldest inns in Peterborough. The public house was re-established in Bridge Street during the 19th century. It was demolished in 1966 and eventually the Magistrates Court - opened by the Queen in March 1978 - replaced it.

Below: One of Peterborough's main shopping streets, this view of Bridge Street takes in Mac Fisheries (a chain which is still a well known name today), Wards, Woolworths - and the new Marks and Spencer, which was in the process of being built at the time. A sharp eye might be able to pick out a sign indicating the Grand Hotel in the background, where at the time lunch would have cost you between five and thirteen shillings and evening dinner was only a little more expensive. Their weekly tariff was 17 guineas; younger readers will appreciate the information that a guinea was one pound and one shilling (5p). In the first half of the 20th century Woolworths stores were known around the country as the place to shop if you happened to be a bit hard up. With their goods on offer at bargain prices, the store was invaluable during the dark days of depression and unemployment. Woolworths started their life in Britain as 'Woolworths 3d and 6d Stores', a name that was a direct echo of the original '5 and 10 cent Stores' that spread in a chain across America at the end of the 19th Century. F W Woolworth, who in 1879 opened his first stores selling a wide range of goods at fixed low prices, had a chain of over 1,000 shops in the USA by 1911. With his brother C S Woolworth he later expanded into the UK, Canada and Europe.

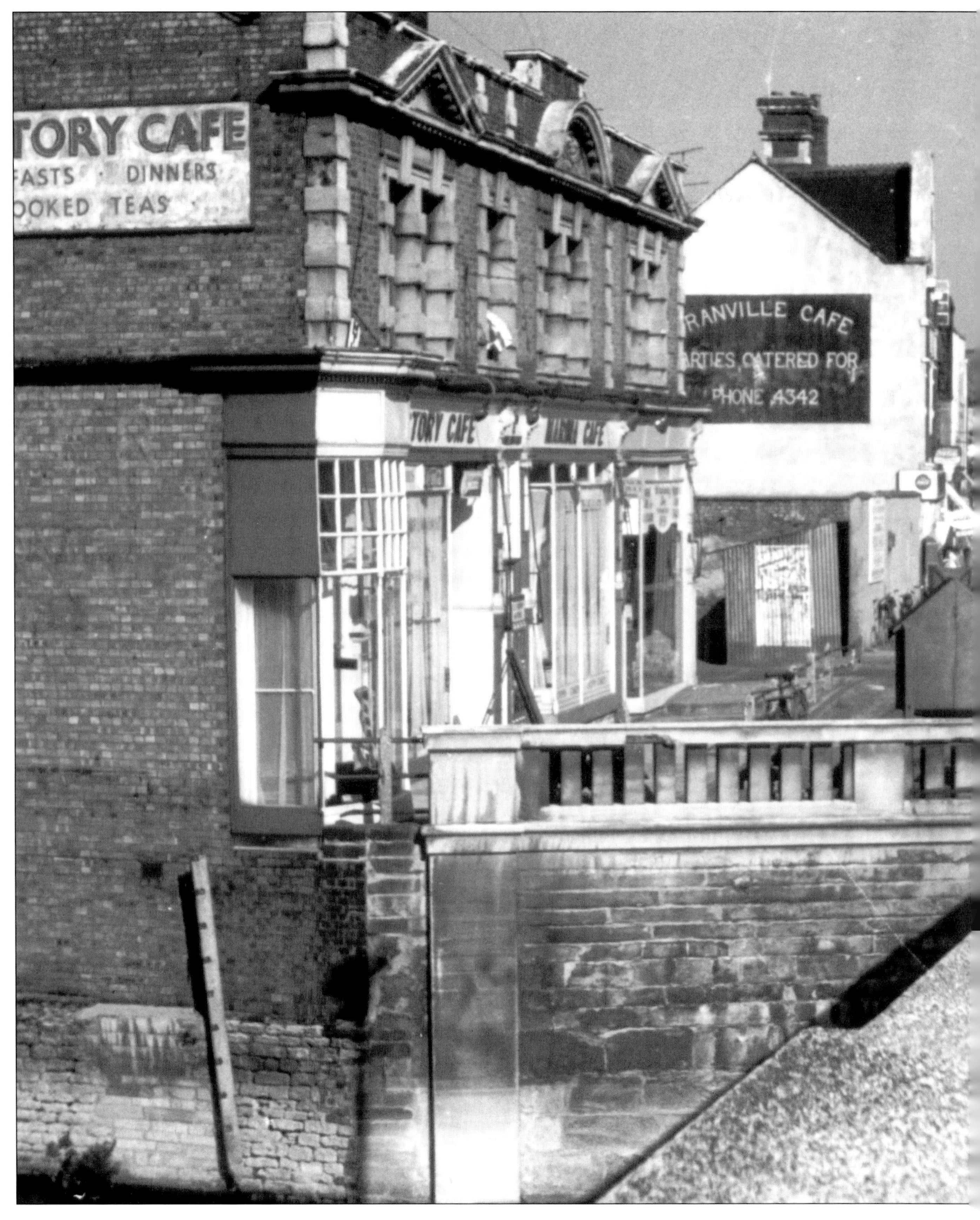

The Victory Cafe, whose unusual name points to the cafe having been opened in 1945, was just one of a number of businesses that had occupied this building during its long life. It was at one time the Central Temperance Hotel. By the 1880s the Temperance Society, which stood out against strong drink of all kinds, was flourishing in many places - the late 19th and early 20th century was the heyday of the movement. There was a reaction among church people (particularly the Society of Friends, or Quakers) to the influence of the 'demon drink', and around the country they opened up 'dry' hotels and restaurants, provided towns with fresh water fountains and even coffee carts that toured the streets to provide people with an alternative in liquid refreshment. The Temperance Hotel in Bridge Street was popular with men visiting the city on business.

It was a sunny day when the photographer snapped this view some time in the 1960s, and Bridge Street was crowded with shoppers (who don't appear to be patronising the Victory Cafe - or its near neighbour and rival the Granville Cafe). There are far more pedestrians than cars around in this busy scene, pointing to this perhaps being a Saturday, the traditional shopping day for workers and housewives alike.

A glance at the 1930s

HOT OFF THE PRESS

The years of the 1930s saw Adolph Hitler's sickening anti-Jewish campaign echoed in the streets of Britain. On 19th October 1936 Oswald Mosley's 7,000-strong British Union of Fascists clashed head on with thousands of Jews and Communists in London, resulting in 80 people being injured in the ensuing battle. Mosley and his 'blackshirts' later rampaged through the streets beating up Jews and smashing the windows of their businesses.
A dark day in our country's history.

THE WORLD AT LARGE

In India, Gandhi's peaceful protests against British rule were gathering momentum. The Salt Laws were a great bone of contention: forced to buy salt from the British government, thousands of protestors marched to the salt works, intending to take it over in the name of the Indian people. Policemen and guards attacked the marchers, but not one of them fought back. Gandhi, who earned for himself the name 'Mahatma' - Great Soul - was assassinated in 1948.

ROYAL WATCH

The talking point of the early 1930s was the affair of the Prince of Wales, who later became King Edward VIII, and American divorcee Wallis Simpson. Faced with a choice, Edward gave up his throne for 'the woman I love' and spent the remainder of his life in exile. Many supported him, though they might not have been as keen to do so if they had been aware of his Nazi sympathies, kept strictly under wraps at the time.

The 1960s were years of massive development in Peterborough, and the crane that towers above the buildings in the background speaks volumes about the old and familiar streets and buildings we lost - and also about the wonderful new facilities we gained. A large sign outside Petts & Co tells us that a box junction - a new concept at the time - had been placed at the end of Bridge Street. A familiar sight today, back then we needed the sign as a reminder of what box junctions were all about - keeping the roads clear of vehicles that often blocked a right turn when the traffic lights changed, obstructing the flow of traffic. This long line of cars in the right-hand lane would appear to be waiting their turn. How long did they have to wait, we wonder? By the 1960s traffic was becoming a problem in Peterborough, and car ownership was set to double during the next 20 years. In the years that followed the second world war few ordinary people could afford to buy a family car, and car ownership remained an unattainable dream until post-war prosperity began to become a reality in the mid 1950s. Traffic problems were not only Peterborough's; between 1953 and 1963 the number of cars in the country had risen from one car for every twenty-four people to one for every seven.

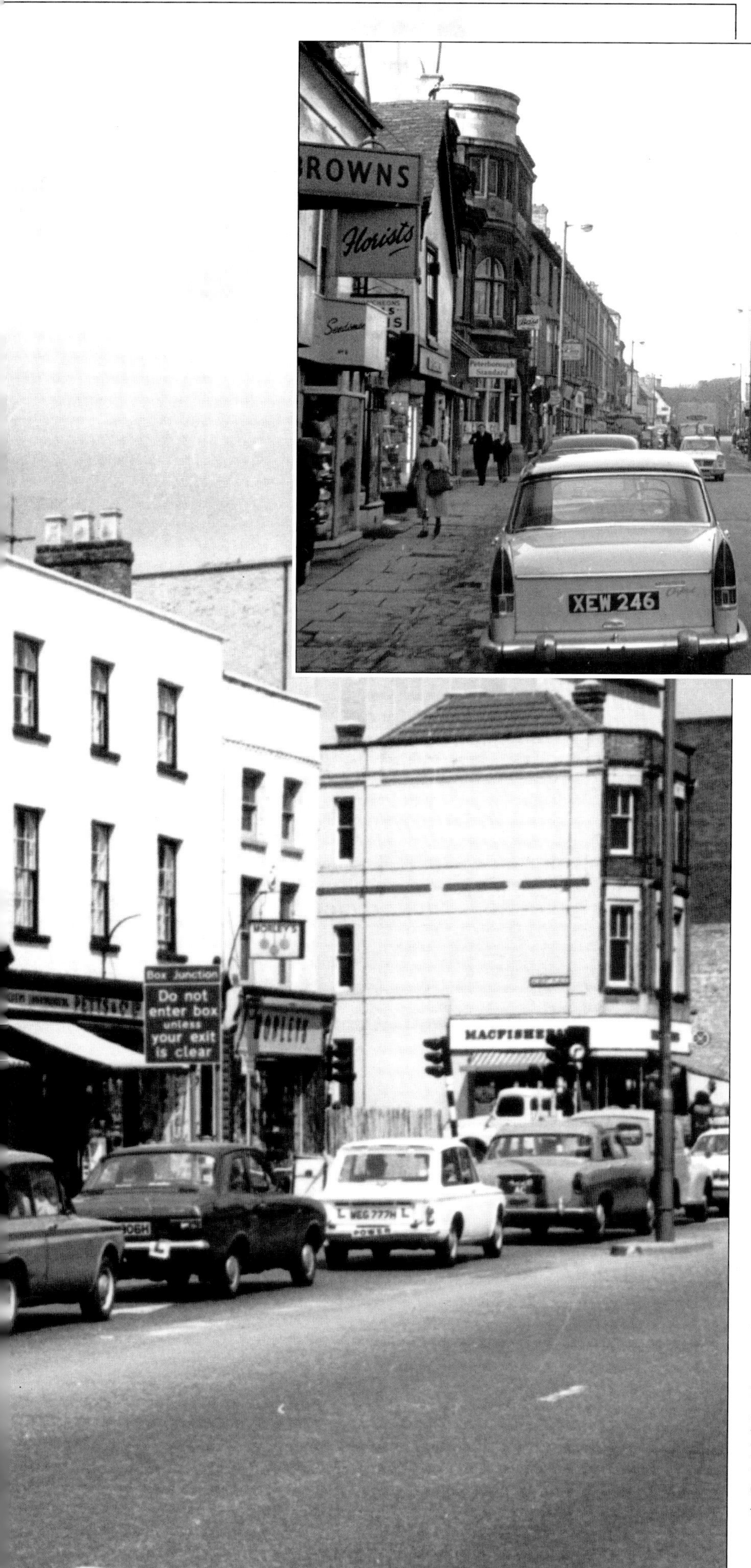

Above: Dancing the night away was as popular in the 1950s and 60s as it is today - except that during the 1950s you would have danced in your partner's arms! As enthusiasm for rock 'n roll and jiving began to wane, and bands like the Beatles and the Rolling Stones took over from Elvis Presley and Buddy Holly, dancing separately came into vogue. Not so much fun for those who like to dance with their partners rather than alongside them! This dance hall on the right of Church Street was once the Corn Exchange, which itself had replaced Peterborough's very first playhouse and theatre. It was later demolished and the site redeveloped; the central Post Office and an insurance company were eventually built there. W & J Brown, nurseryman, had their premises on the opposite side of the road. Well-known to the gardeners of Peterborough, the shop was eventually acquired by Brown Brothers, butchers (no family connection). Further along, and directly opposite the dance hall, were the offices of the Peterborough Standard; a sharp eye might pick out the sign above the doorway.

R. J.

The normally busy roads are very quiet in this 1960s view of Long Causeway from Cathedral Square. A couple of cars, a bus and a motor cycle and sidecar (how long is it since you saw one?) constitutes the only traffic in this tranquil scene, and the customary few blokes hang around the newsagents stand by the Gates Memorial. A tall crane on the right stands tall above the surrounding buildings, informing us that construction work of the Hereward Centre is going on out of sight.
Of special interest is the little Mini Traveller on the right, still cherished today by the many affectionate owners who managed to hang on to theirs.

The Mini was introduced to British drivers in 1959 by Alexander Issigonis (who also developed the popular Morris Minor) in response to Germany's popular VW Beetle. The Mini's transverse engine made it possible to seat four passengers in comfort in spite of the car only being an incredible ten feet in length. The little vehicle was practical, affordable and fuel-efficient - all features that helped to establish it as a firm favourite, especially with the student population and other hard-up younger drivers. Issigonis was knighted in 1969 for his contribution to British design, and by the time he died in 1988 more than five million Minis had been sold.

A wide expanse of old cobbles still survives in this late 1950s view of Cumbergate. The Ford Popular on the left will bring back a lot of memories for Peterborian motorists who were driving at the time. But do you remember the even earlier model? There was a characterful little car for you.... Do you remember the strange layout of the gears, with reverse where first gear would be on other cars? Double de-clutching into first gear? And the hand-brake below the dashboard? And the vacuum wipers that gave up when you put your foot down and flogged away like mad when you eased off the accelerator? Motoring ain't what it was! By way of contrast, note the long, sleek lines of the Vauxhall Cresta on the right, its 'American limo' shape looking just a little out of place in this conservatively English view of Cumbergate. Crates of bottles are being delivered to the Greyhound, which was one of a total of seven public houses in this short stretch of roadway. The premises of Watkins & Stafford, who were a well-known furnishing firm in Peterborough, can be seen on the right. Cumbergate has a long history; the house of correction was once situated here, demolished in 1844. The street was also the site of some of the city's almshouses, built in 1903 by a legacy from Miss Frances Pears.

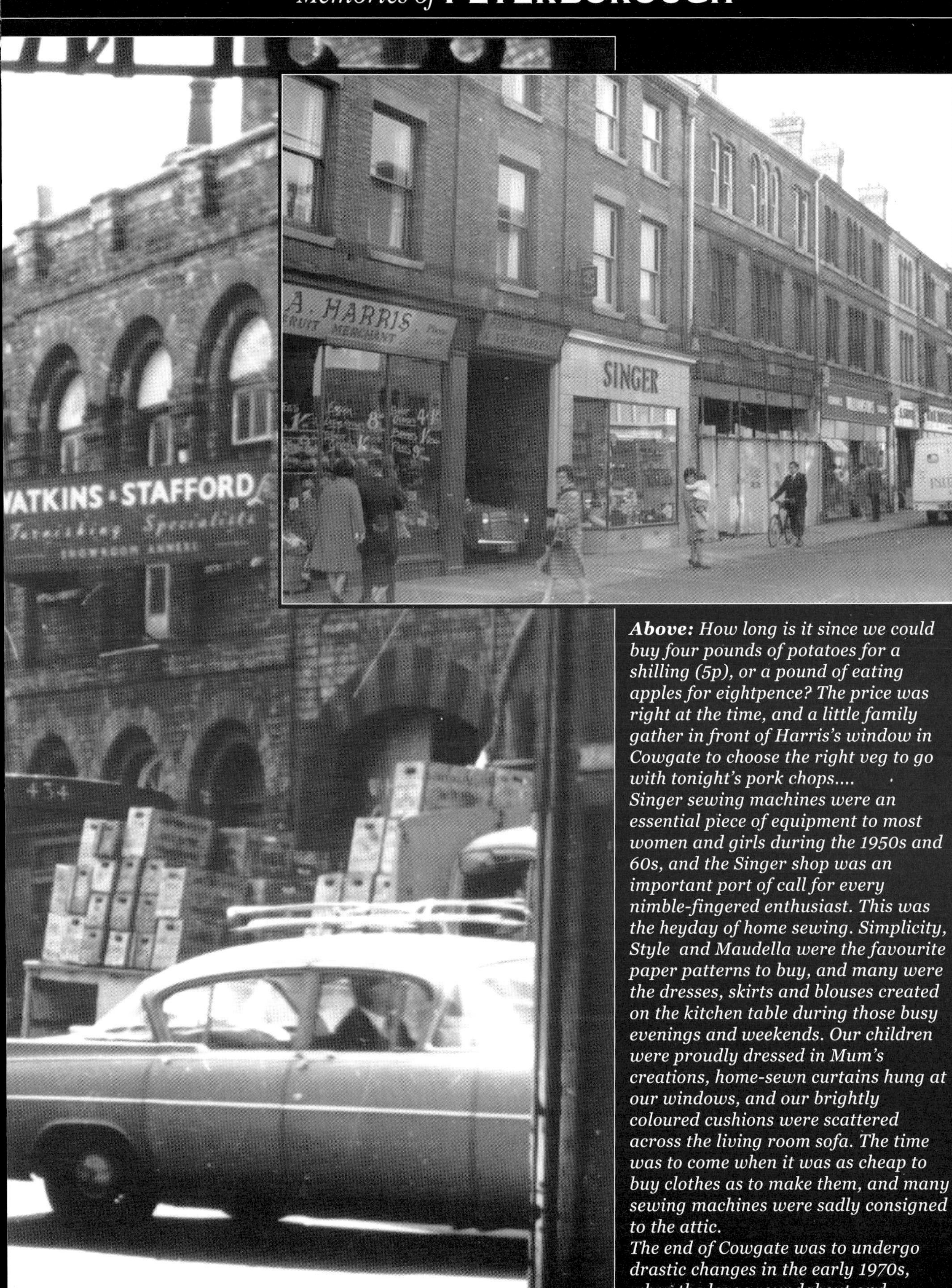

Above: *How long is it since we could buy four pounds of potatoes for a shilling (5p), or a pound of eating apples for eightpence? The price was right at the time, and a little family gather in front of Harris's window in Cowgate to choose the right veg to go with tonight's pork chops....*
Singer sewing machines were an essential piece of equipment to most women and girls during the 1950s and 60s, and the Singer shop was an important port of call for every nimble-fingered enthusiast. This was the heyday of home sewing. Simplicity, Style and Maudella were the favourite paper patterns to buy, and many were the dresses, skirts and blouses created on the kitchen table during those busy evenings and weekends. Our children were proudly dressed in Mum's creations, home-sewn curtains hung at our windows, and our brightly coloured cushions were scattered across the living room sofa. The time was to come when it was as cheap to buy clothes as to make them, and many sewing machines were sadly consigned to the attic.
The end of Cowgate was to undergo drastic changes in the early 1970s, when the large roundabout and subways we know today were constructed to form part of Bourges Boulevard - positioned on land that at one time was the city's burial ground.

A glance at the 1930s

MELODY MAKERS

Throughout the 1930s a young American trombonist called Glenn Miller was making his mark in the world of music. By 1939 the Glenn Miller sound was a clear leader in the field; his clean-cut, meticulously executed arrangements of numbers such as 'A String of Pearls' and 'Moonlight Serenade' brought him fame across the world as a big-band leader. During a flight to England from Paris in 1944 Miller's plane disappeared; no wreckage was ever found.

What's new?

With no driving tests or speed restrictions, 120,000 people were killed on the roads in Britain between the two world wars. In 1934 a Halifax man, Percy Shaw, invented a safety device destined to become familiar the world over: reflecting roadstuds. In dark or foggy conditions the studs that reflected light from the car's headlights kept traffic on the 'straight and narrow' and must over the years have saved many lives.

SCIENCE AND DISCOVERY

By observing the heavens, astronomers had long believed that there in the constellation of Gemini lay a new planet, so far undiscovered. They began to search for the elusive planet, and a special astronomical camera was built for the purpose. The planet Pluto was discovered by amateur astronomer Clyde Tombaugh in 1930, less than a year later.

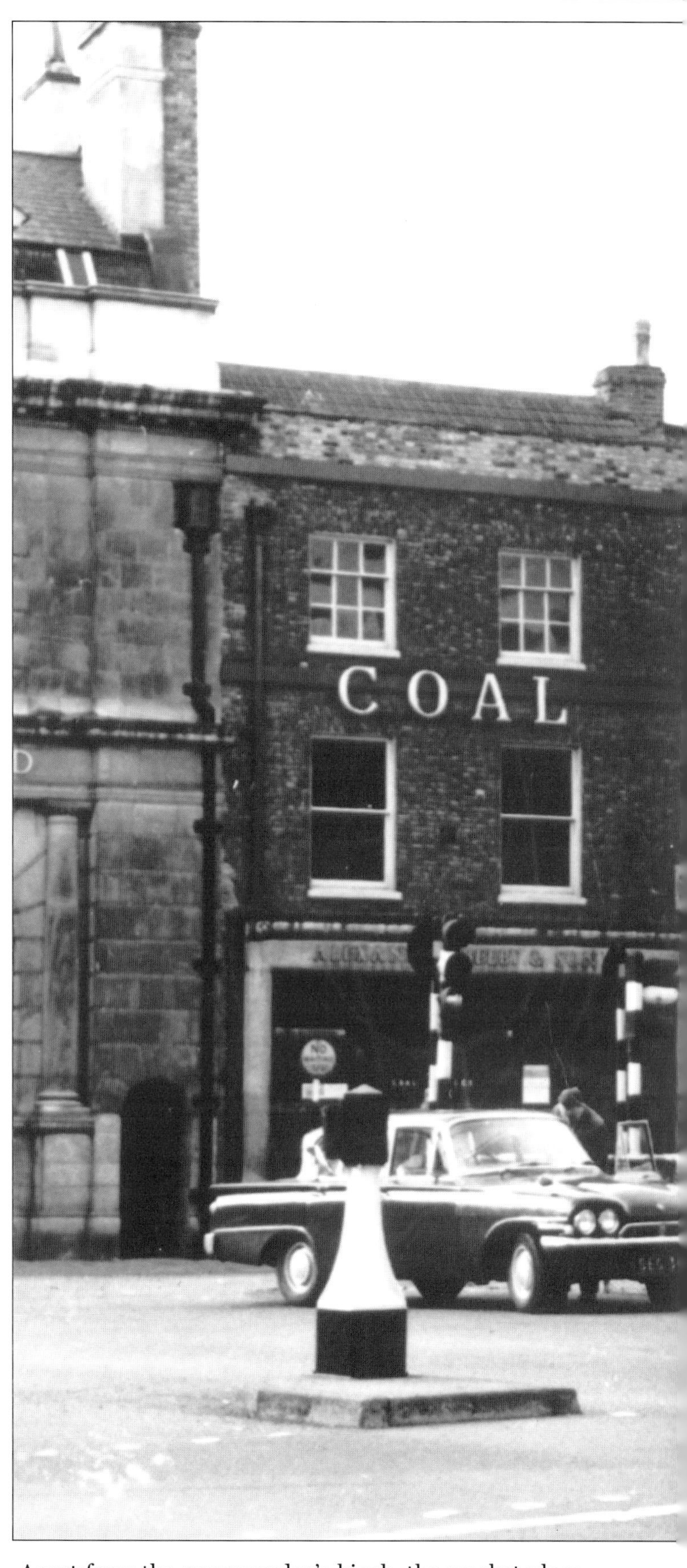

Apart from the news vendor's kiosk, the market place was deserted when this photograph was taken, and the Gates Memorial dominates the scene. The memorial was a familiar landmark in Peterborough for many years before it was removed from its traditional position to be ignominiously deposited in Bishop Road Gardens minus its taps, basins and plinth. The memorial was a gift to the city from the widow of Henry

Pearson Gates, the city's Chief Magistrate and first Mayor of Peterborough under the Charter of 1874 (the newly elected council's unanimous choice). On his death in 1893 his widow had the beautiful monument - which also doubled as a useful drinking fountain - made to honour his memory. Its removal was a sad loss to many Peterborians.
At the time of the photograph, traffic was a part of city life that was simply taken for granted. Pedestrian areas were undreamed of back then, and the 'Keep Left' signs were needed at this spot. The lack of traffic in this scene would perhaps indicate that this was a Sunday; the doors of the Peterborough Building Society are fast shut, though we cannot see whether Timothy Whites - later taken over by the giant Boots - is open or closed.

Above: A scene that is familiar yet so different! The names above the shops have changed, of course, and today we would see the Norwich & Peterborough Building Society, First Sport, the Bakers Oven, Hughes TV and Burger King occupying these positions. Sadly, a modern building now houses Barclays Bank, though its position is unchanged - and thankfully the loos are still in the same place! These characterful market booths have long disappeared from Cathedral Square, and since it was opened in October 1963 the new undercover market has wormed its way into our affections, and today is so much a part of the life of the city that we couldn't imagine being without it. It has so much to offer us, with dozens of stalls offering thousands of goodies, from confectionery to cosmetics.

The Guildhall, which was used as a Town Hall for many years, and the parish church form a fitting background to the scene, as they have for many years, though St John's had a spire when it was first built. By the 1820s the spire was judged to be unsafe and it was subsequently demolished. A keystone on the middle arch at the front of the Guildhall, or Butter Cross, informs us that the building dates back to 1671. It was used as a market hall right up to 1926, when butter, eggs, cheese and other local produce was brought in from the outlying farms to be sold by the womenfolk. Until 1842 the upper room was used as a magistrates court.

Above right: A fascinating story was breaking on the day this photograph was taken, and the Sunday Express carried 'The secret story of a prince's courtship'. As the photograph is undated, speculating about the prince in question can only be a stab in the dark. It was in the 1950s that Prince Rainier of Monaco married the film actress Grace Kelly. No wonder he fell for the star - her remarkable beauty won her fans and followers across the world. But would their romance fit the headline? An alternative would perhaps have been a re-hash of the exiled King Edward VIII's abdication story. His affair with and subsequent marriage to American divorcee Wallis Simpson hit every headline during the 1930s, and as further details about the couple came to light over the years, their romantic story was sure to attract readers, many of whom sympathised and thought that they should at least have been allowed to live in England. There were further secrets, however, that even the press were not aware of at the time; only in recent years was the couple's sympathy with Hitler's Nazi creed brought to light. Whatever the story published that day, a number of punters (all male!) are patronising the news stand. The man on the left seems to be gripped by the story - or is he simply checking the football results?

Right: Knee length boots, long hair and mini skirts were badges of the 1960s and psychedelic purples, shocking pinks and brash yellows were in and the tight perms and flowing skirts of the previous decade were most definitely out. This was the heyday of boutiques such as this establishment on the left in Westgate.
Rubbing shoulders with the fashion culture of the 60s was that rather more conservative concern, Kendall. Kendall, of course, had nothing to do with short skirts and long boots; the product they specialised in was very fine showerproof and waterproof outer wear, and their well known catchphrase 'Kendall keeps you dry' would have been well-known even to the skimpily-clad younger generation. Westgate was already marked out with the double yellow lines that prevented kerbside parking, though on the day of the photograph, traffic along what is one of the oldest roads in Peterborough was very light. The origin of the name 'Westgate' is a bit of a mystery as the road does not lead towards the west. It has been suggested that it might have once been 'Webstergate' (weavers' street). Westgate remains home to a number of well known city centre pubs, notably The Bull, The Royal (now the Tut and Shive), the Wortley's Almshouses (allegedly used by Charles Dickens as a model for the workhouse in 'Oliver Twist'), and, of course, the Brewery Tap - Peterborough's only brewery.

Below: As far as the younger ladies are concerned, spring has arrived; time to bring out the lightweight coats, white shoes and matching white handbags. The old lady on the right, however, is biding her time, no doubt brought up to believe in the old adage 'Ne'er cast a clout till May is out'. But it looks set fair to be a beautiful day in Cathedral Square, though the actual date of the photograph is unknown.
The square is dominated today - as it has been for hundreds of years - by Christianity as well as commerce. The market no longer exists, of course, but Cathedral Square has emerged through all the recent changes as a blend of old traditional businesses and modern department stores, many linked to the Queensgate shopping centre by way of arcades. And over the entire scene the Cathedral presides, as it has since it was consecrated in 1238. Henry VIII's much wronged first wife, Catherine of Aragon, is buried here. Around the country, many were secretly in sympathy with the poor lady who was divorced by the King because she failed to give Henry the son he wanted (though only a few brave souls dared to say so, and paid for it with their lives). A portrait of the 16th century gravedigger, Robert Scarlett, who buried Catherine still hangs in the nave.

Nose to tail, a long line of traffic moves a yard or two at a time past the Co-op building along Westgate. In earlier decades the number of pedestrians around the city streets far outnumbered the cars, but we can see that by the late 1960s the situation has been reversed. The gleaming Triumph Vitesse, the Vauxhall Viva following closely behind, and the Humber Sceptre take us on a 30-year journey back through time. The A40 further along the queue is a long way from its original home ground - it bears an Anglesey registration. The Humber Sceptre - from the Rootes Group - will be familiar to those of our readers who were lucky enough to own one, or who envied those who owned one. Favoured by bank managers and hospital consultants, this splendid motor sported a classy wooden interior trim, extra driving lights at the front and a slightly different radiator based on the Hillman Super Minx.

We can see from the shop facade on the right that the typical 1960s 'square block' architecture was by this time influencing the city's traditional early 20th century (and even earlier) buildings. Many of the older buildings in Westgate have been demolished and new shopping experiences such as the Queensgate Centre have added gloss and glitz to the old thoroughfare.

In earlier days the number of pedestrians around the city streets outnumbered the cars

All the fun of the fair!

You should see the sights I see, when I'm...taking a peep into the big top! This group of little girls might not have managed to get in to see the show, but they were determined to see it anyway, and their resourcefulness paid off. Coming across a set of loose tent lacings was too good an opportunity to miss, and the girls were soon enjoying a free show. The problem was, of course, that they couldn't all see at the same time! Having been nicely brought up, however, these little girls (are the two wearing light coats and caps on the right twins?) are not pushing and shoving, but are patiently waiting to take their turn at the gap in the canvas.

But wouldn't it be nice if we, too, could take a peep and find out what was so fascinating? The antics of a couple of clowns, perhaps, or a line of long-legged dancing girls. Alas, we will never know.

It would be fascinating, too, to know what became of these girls, who will very likely be mothers and grandmothers, and will have passed the big five-o. What kind of careers did they carve out for themselves, we wonder? We must hope that life has been good to them.

A glance at the 1940s

WHAT'S ON?

In wartime Britain few families were without a wireless set. It was the most popular form of entertainment, and programmes such as ITMA, Music While You Work and Mrs Dale's Diary provided the people with an escape from the harsh realities of bombing raids and ration books. In 1946 the BBC introduced the Light Programme, the Home Service and the Third Programme, which gave audiences a wider choice of listening.

GETTING AROUND

October 1948 saw the production of Britain's first new car designs since before the war. The Morris Minor was destined for fame as one of the most popular family cars, while the four-wheel-drive Land Rover answered the need for a British-made off-road vehicle. The country was deeply in the red, however, because of overseas debts incurred during the war. The post-war export drive that followed meant that British drivers had a long wait for their own new car.

SPORTING CHANCE

American World Heavyweight Boxing Champion Joe Louis, who first took the title back in 1937, ruled the world of boxing during, making a name for himself 1940s as unbeatable. Time after time he successfully defended his title against all comers, finally retiring in 1948 after fighting an amazing 25 title bouts throughout his boxing career. Louis died in 1981 at the age of 67.

Who was the over-optimistic fairground ride designer of old who invented the name 'dodgem' cars? As we all know from personal experience, 'dodging 'em' never has played a part in this popular ride. Admit it - ramming 'em is a lot more fun! Round and round the floor the kids went, their journey punctuated by bangs and crashes as their own rubber bumper made violent contact with someone else's rubber bumper. Mini

traffic jams that called for the services of the long-suffering attendant to separate the jammed up cars were all part of the fun. And didn't those attendants seem daring when we were children? Nonchalantly stepping from car to car as they dished out tickets and small change, very often with a cigarette dangling from their lips, they took the risk of bumps, bruises and broken legs literally in their stride.

For many of these children having a wonderful time at Perkins' Sports and Family Day in June 1957, this would have been their first experience behind the wheel, and the experience perhaps sparked off a longing for the time when they would be old enough to sit behind the steering wheel of a full-size car.

CORONA

Perkins were well known in Peterborough as a caring company who looked after their workforce. This included involving employees in various competitions, sports fixtures and projects such as their highly successful suggestions scheme. Even in the early days of the company it was a competition that brought about the original logo from which Perkins' famous square and four circles evolved - a little different in purpose from the 'Miss Perkins' beauty contest! In 1951 the company became involved in the Festival of Britain, when Perkins engines were on display. The year 1953, however, was not only the year of the Queen's coronation but it was the firm's red letter year as far as special events went. The Sports and Family day was celebrated on 12th June, while 4th September marked the occasion of the company's 21st birthday. Swings, roundabouts and rides for the children of their employees were par for the course, and even a ride on the factory's auto truck was enjoyed, specially by the boys. *(overleaf)* Thousands of employees converged on the fairground which, like fairgrounds the world over, had an atmosphere of its very own that had to be experienced to be

Continued overleaf

From previous page

appreciated; the whirr and hum of the rides, the loud beat of the music, several different tunes fighting with each other for attention, and the squeals of the girls as they spun dizzily around on the speedway ride *(previous page)*.
No anniversary is complete without the opportunity to eat, and the fairground would most probably have had its toffee apples, dark red and shining as if they had been varnished, shocking pink candy floss that was spun around a stick while you waited, paper bags of crunchy brandy snap and lots of ice cream (perhaps from Stapletons?), in tubs, cornets or wafers.

30
Lister
AUTO TRUCK
SWL 2 TON
EC 6035

Both pictures: It was the Big Day - 4th September 1953 - the day that young and not-so-young had all been waiting for. And the event being celebrated? Perkins' 21st anniversary, and the company had really gone to town on the festivities that marked their coming of age. By this time Perkins' Eastfield factory had around 3,500 employees on their payroll, so this was a big occasion in more than one sense. Events of one kind and another had been staged during an entire week of festivities that were laid on for the company's dealers, suppliers and customers. On the Saturday of that week it was the employees' turn, and a great day out was planned for the workers and their families. A funfair complete with stalls and children's rides was part of the day's fun, and under the watchful eye of their parents the kids set out to have a whale of a time.

The 'switchback' ride *(below)* was a little less hairy than Nemesis or The Corkscrew, and it obviously require a certain amount of parent power to get it running. But the kids loved it, and we can imagine that the queue for this particular attraction would have been a long one. We draw a veil over the enthusiasm of these dads, however, who would have gone home at the end of the day looking forward to a long soak in a hot Radox bath....

But this was, after all, the children's day, full of fun, happiness and laughter - except from the little boy who doesn't appear to be enjoying his ride on the roundabout very much! *(right)* Looking far more cheerful was nine-year-old Sylvia Cooke, who had fallen victim to that scourge of former years, the dreaded polio. Polio was a major disease of the time, visiting children and leaving behind its terrible mark of wasted and useless limbs. Young Sylvia was unaware that in America Jonas Edward Salk was already studying the disease with a view to producing a safe and effective vaccine, though it would be another year before a mass field trial was held. His new vaccine was released in the United States in April 1955, though further research continued and in 1960 an oral vaccine was developed. The vaccines brought the disease under control and today polio is rarely seen.

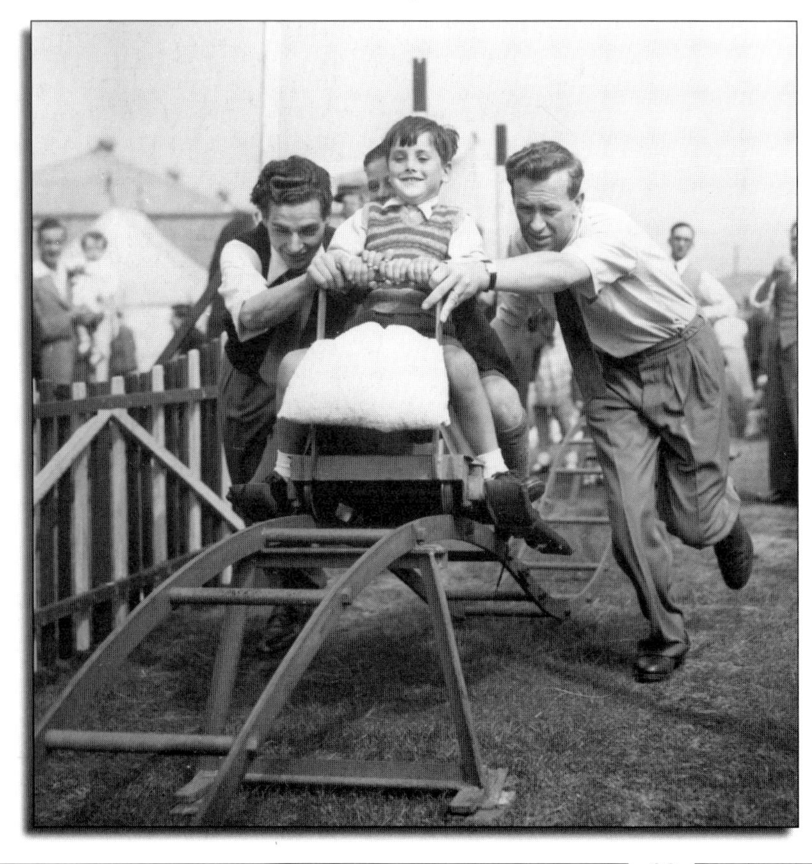

On the move

The Nash was a large, late 1940s American car, distinguished for us by the unusual white decoration on its front mudguards. When the Nash was produced, motor car design had changed little since the austere designs of wartime; during World War II - and for a number of years afterwards - design stood still as manufacturers drew breath and prepared for the future.

In Britain particularly the years of the second world war had not been easy ones for those businesses involved in the motor trade. The chronic shortage of parts, petrol rationing, and the almost total absence of new cars (Vauxhall, for example, only produced around 100 cars between 1939 and 1946) all combined to make things difficult for garage owners. Even towards the end of the 1940s the effects of the war were still being felt, and certain goods remained in short supply. This included the motor car, as new cars were being exported as fast as they came off the production line.

This photograph dates from 1953, however, and by that time changes in car design were imminent. Mudguards and running boards like those on the 'sit up and beg' design of the Nash were set to become a thing of the past; headlights would be faired-in and incorporated into sleeker body lines, flashing indicators would replace the semaphore type (remember how easy it was to forget them and leave them sticking out?), and even quarter-light windows would gradually disappear from our cars.

This marvellous Humber Super Snipe seems to have been the only vehicle waiting for the traffic lights in Market Place to flip to green, and was caught on camera as the driver turned into Long Causeway. The Super Snipe, a top British luxury saloon, was a car that was aspired to by Peterborians who had a bob or two to spend on the better things in life, and the lovely motor would have turned a few heads as it made its stately way through the streets of the city. The year of the photograph was 1953 - the year of the Queen's coronation, though as the month was October the flags and bunting had long ago been packed away in lofts and attics, and those wild and wonderful parties and dances had become a distant memory. The shops and businesses that make up the background to this picture will be familiar to many readers: Alexander Beeby; Timothy Whites when it had 'And Taylor' added to its title; Kendall's umbrellas, and Kammer's sweets and tobacco shop, advising passers-by that 'Players Please'. A number of vehicles are parked along the kerb, hopefully outside the 'No Waiting Here' restrictions. Spot the truck almost hidden behind the Humber, piled high with parcels. Was this perhaps a GPO delivery?

Above: The destination of the gleaming Humber is revealed - the Bull Hotel in Westgate. Perhaps its driver is meeting clients for lunch in the Bull's rather nice grill room?
The logo proudly worn on the Super Snipe's radiator informs us that the car has been fitted with a Perkins engine. The story of the famous logo began with a competition that was staged by the company in its early years; the prize was £15 - a large sum of money back then. Unfortunately the winning entry had to be withdrawn because it too closely resembled someone else's emblem. (Did the winner also have to return the £15, we wonder?) Perkins' familiar square and four circles logo (symbolic of four different diesel applications) was devised in the 1930s. The Super Snipe was an example of monocoque construction, and had no separate chassis. In the early 1950s the predominant colour of cars was still black, though things were about to change in a big way as vehicles produced in lighter colours began to roll off the production lines.
Humber was of course part of the Rootes group which disappeared when the company was absorbed by Chrysler.

BUSES

Left: A trip down Memory Lane that will take many readers back to those draughty days of old, when catching a bus meant queuing in the Bishops Road bus station - a very different place from today's modern bus terminus in Queensgate shopping centre. The bus station was quiet when this view was captured , with only a couple of passengers in the background patiently waiting to get home. These original open sided shelters gave little protection from the elements, so waiting around for a bus could be a very chilly experience. Peterborough has had its public transport since the turn of the 20th century, when horse-drawn omnibuses carried passengers into the city and home again. The first electric trams were introduced in January 1903, and tracks were laid to Newark, Walton and Dogsthorpe. Inevitably, motor buses eventually took over from the trams and by the mid-1920s the Peterborough Electric Traction Company were running the first of their double-decker buses. A merger with the Eastern Counties Omnibus Co followed, and the company bought out many local bus operators. In its heyday the company's routes covered around 500 miles, and their fleet numbered 77 buses. Many were sad to see the old bus station in Bishops Road demolished, but the warmth and convenience of the new Queensgate facility, opened in 1982, went a long way towards compensating travellers for its loss. The Magistrates Court was built on the site of the old bus station.

Above: Neither pedestrians nor traffic are out and about in the market place, and this scooter rider has found time to sit for a few minutes to flick through his newspaper. Is he fascinated by the News of the World's report on 'The truth about wrestling and muscle men'? Or is he perhaps captivated by a glamorous pin-up in the Daily Mirror? We will never know, though it is interesting to speculate.... In the background The Greyhound and its next door neighbour the Bell and Oak have something to please most Peterborians, one offering Bass and the other, Double Diamond. Double Diamond has been working wonders since the slogan was thought up in the early 1950s. What turned the catchphrase into one of the best-known beer adverts of all time was the singing of the little ditty to the tune of 'There's a hole in my bucket'. Readers could probably sing it now if hard pressed!

The Wimpy Bar would have proved very popular at closing time, when drinkers only needed to walk a few steps to get a tasty supper. Since this photograph was taken, the Queensgate shopping centre has added its own special appeal to the city. Few other shopping centres can boast comfortable, nicely-carpeted seating areas, water features and 80-odd shops all under one roof.

The power to move the World

Frank Perkins was the son of a Victorian engineer - he was also the grandson of Thomas Perkins, who in 1872 had gone into partnership with William Barford to form the Peterborough engineering firm of Barford & Perkins. In its early days, Barford & Perkins showed an interest in innovative applications of automotive power; its 1896 catalogues featured the revolutionary steam powered ploughing and traction engines which, at £600 each, represented a considerable investment at a time when many leisured people lived in quiet comfort on such an annual income. By 1904 the firm was manufacturing one of the earliest motor driven road rollers. The family tradition for engineering invention was already established, and it was left for Frank to carry on with the work which was to revolutionise the motor power of the 20th century.

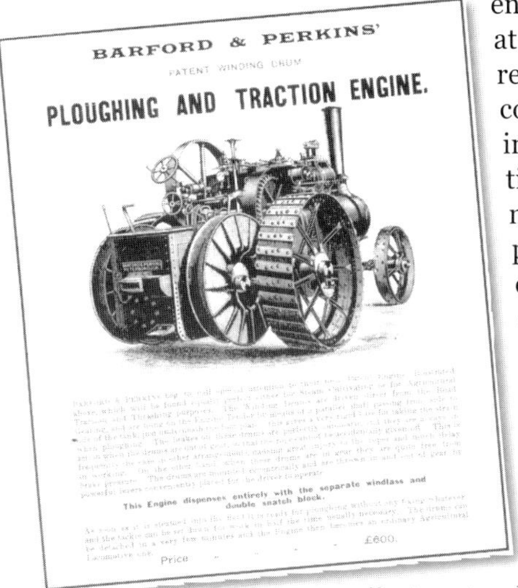

Barford & Perkins became part of the Agricultural & General Engineers (AGE) group in 1919, joining companies such as Aveling & Porter of Rochester. They worked together to fit their equipment with diesel engines (from 1927 on), and to support this work Frank Perkins engaged designer Charles Chapman as his personal assistant. Unfortunately the Great Depression which followed the Wall Street crash of 1929 led to drastic consolidation which resulted in Frank Perkins and Charles Chapman losing their jobs.

The pair had the option of taking over a Sevenoaks laundry, but instead they preferred to hang their faith - and their private money - on developing high speed diesel engines. At a time when diesel engines were too heavy and cumbersome for anything but large, slow-moving vehicles, these two men had a vision that small diesel engines could be produced which would be suitable for 30 cwt (one and a half ton) trucks, small vans and private cars. One day in March 1932 they spent time together working out designs and business plans on the backs of letters and old envelopes - and the same evening were involved in a road accident which almost put an end to their plans.

Left: *An advertisement dated 1896 for a Barford & Perkins Traction Engine.*
Bottom Left: *Frank Perkins, founder of the modern Company.*
Below: *The 'P' Series engine production line in 1947.*
Facing page: *Number 17 Queen Street, the first registered office of F. Perkins Ltd.*

Frank Perkins, an enterprising and forceful salesman, was confident that he could raise the £10,000 necessary to keep the new company afloat for the two years they envisaged it would take to get into production. He approached his brother-in-law Alan Richardson and G D Perks, a former Vice-Chairman of AGE, to contribute funds and join him (as MD at a salary of £750 a year) and Charles Chapman (as Technical Director on £546) as co-directors of F Perkins Ltd. The firm leased part of the old Barford & Perkins works in Queen Street, Peterborough for £75 pa where Norman Burney and three other ex-Aveling & Porter men joined them at seventy five shillings (£3.75p) a week. Two Peterborough girls completed the workforce of the new born company.

On Saturday (then a working day) 4th December 1932 the very first Perkins diesel engine roared into life, to be baptised in the celebrations at nearby Bay's Wine Bar, the Vixen. Later marques were named Fox, Wolf and Leopard before numbers were introduced as model indication. In January 1933 a Hillman Wizard car had

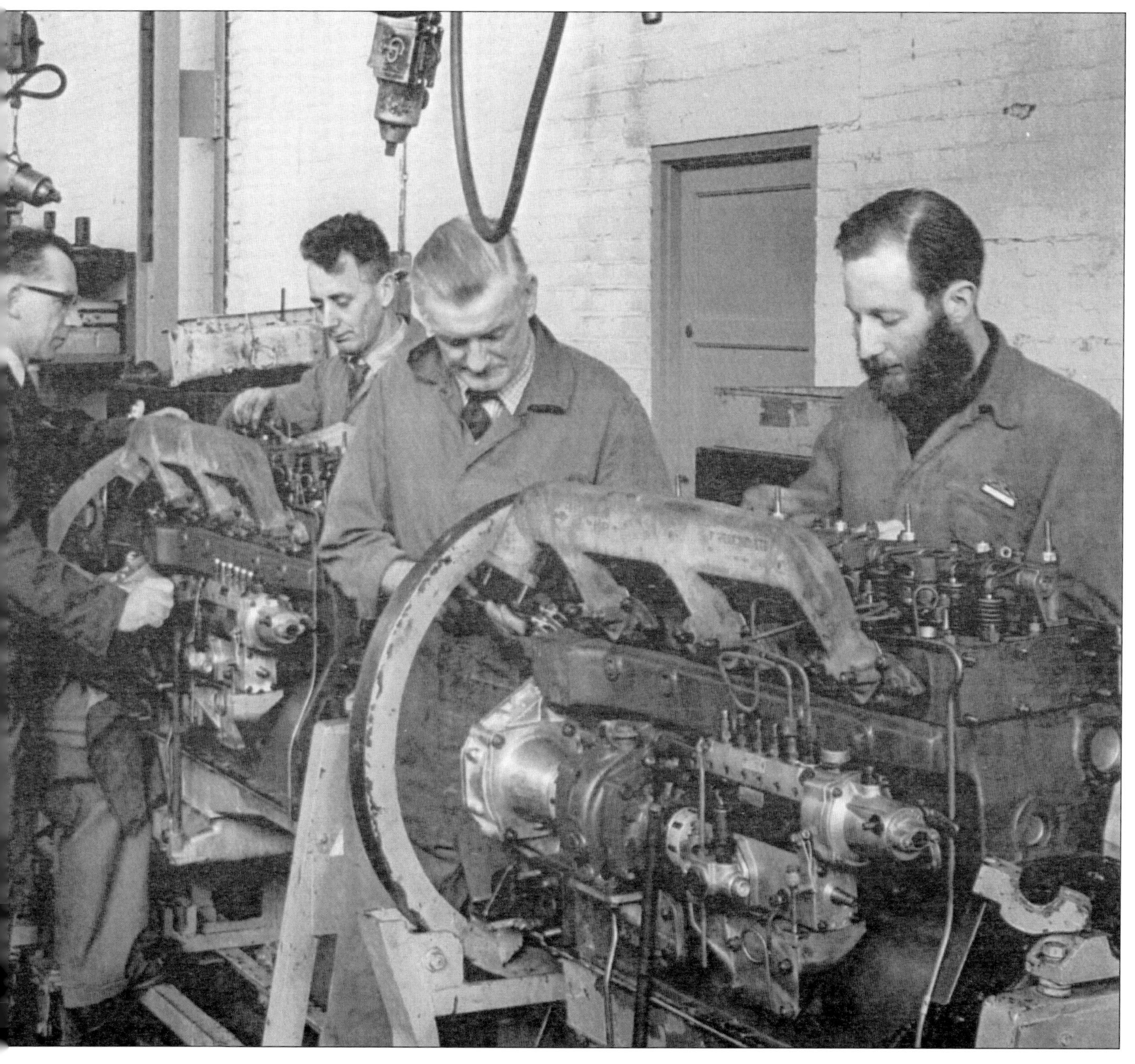

been converted to take one of the first 24 engines, and at the, then, high speed of 50mph became a noted rally winner. The founders even drove to Moscow in a car with a Wolf engine in 1934 to create publicity and in search of business.

When Cyril Kent, with ten years experience as a garage mechanic, joined the firm in 1933 he had fully expected it to go bust within three months, such was the state of many industries in post-Depression Britain, Europe and the USA. History shows how unfounded his fears were. The main thrust of the company in these early years was to convert all sorts of vehicles and motorised machines to diesel. By early 1935 substantial orders were coming in. In March the Commer company ordered eighty Wolves for buses destined for work in India. It is an old public transport tradition in India that as many, if not more, passengers travel on the roof as inside buses and trains. Commer were relying on the three year old company to maintain their reputation in keeping their buses moving for a far longer life span than would ever be expected in England. The engines would be run regardless of heat, slow city traffic held up by sacred cows, rickshaws and ambling crowds, and rugged up-country roads far from the famous Great Trunk Road (known to Kipling's Soldiers Three and other servants of the Raj).

Morale was high at the Perkins expanding works until the 1935 budget slapped the same tax on diesel oil as on petrol, an eight fold increase to 8d (3.5p) per gallon (4 litres). Only the Commer order kept Perkins going as orders for Wolf engines dropped from 110 in the first five months of 1935 to a mere 10 in the four post Budget months, while orders for Leopards went down by over 50percent. Is it any wonder that industrialists call for more businessmen to enter politics? During that troubled year Alan Richardson pumped £20,000 of his own money into Perkins to save it from going under. Compare this veritable fortune with the salaries of directors and staff in the days when small cars cost £100 new and suburban semis could be bought for around seven shillings (35p) a week.

The year 1937, remembered by many as their first

Top: *Engines ready for despatch in the 1940s.*
Above: *The six cylinder 83 b.h.p. engine known as the P6, that was to found the company's fortunes.*
Right: *The entrance to Perkins factory on Queen Street, Peterborough.*

Coronation Year, saw the famous Perkins P6, designed by Charles Chapman, in production. This 83 bhp, six cylinder engine was quieter and smoother than any other diesel the world had seen. It provided the base on which the previously struggling company founded its fortune and it became the highly successful fore-runner of a family of engines used in farming, industrial plants, road building, civil engineering and boats around the world. Originally the series of P6, P4 and P3 engines were to bear the names Panther, Puma and Python respectively but copyright problems led to the replacement of names by numbers.

So successful was the P6 that it outsold the popular Leopard engines and was being offered as the standard power plant by the following famous lorry manufacturers: Albion, Bedford, Commer, Dennis, Dodge, Garner, Guy and Thorneycroft, all were British firms with the exception of American Dodge. During 1936 and 1937 Britain modernised and enlarged her much reduced armed forces so that we could better meet a well prepared enemy. During 1938, with the clouds of war looming on the horizon, the Royal Navy put the P6 through demanding Admiralty Tests to assess its suitability for adoption as a marine engine.

It passed with flying colours and very soon Perkins diesels were fitted in naval launches and tenders, such as the picturesquely nicknamed Green Parrots or admirals' barges, proudly bearing the White Ensign. These adapted engines were the S6 (S for Service) series also used in the fast air sea rescue launches bearing the light blue ensign of the RAF. Remember that the majority of life boats in merchant vessels were then hand powered pulling boats.

By September 1939 Britain was at war with Germany and Perkins' wartime brief from the Government was to produce engines for marine use, and production quickly rose to 1,146 engines in 1941 as the company

Above: *Perkins Australian headquarters at Dandenong in 1950.*
Below: *The typing pool in the 1950s.*

expanded to fill all the buildings in Queen Street. At this time the T12 engine was under development, though the engine was never produced. By 1943 Perkins were working flat out to meet the demands of essential war production - in fact the company's total production during World War II reached an amazing 12,000 engines.

In 1945 hard to win Government approval was granted to Perkins to obtain strictly rationed building materials in order to build a new factory at Eastfield. Planning began in 1945/46 and the factory opened in November 1947. Perkins was then making over 3,000 engines a year. Obviously HMG was looking to rebuilding the war weary industries of Britain and, like Perkins, had an eye to export earnings from a world ravaged by six years of war. Perkins, in common with other British manufacturers of all products, had gone completely over to production of war material but, unlike many others, did not have to make drastic changes to product or plant to do so.

The company confidently faced the post war years knowing that they were the only one who had the ability to produce high speed diesel engines immediately for a world crying out for such engines. There was then no other European factory able to do so, least of all in devastated Germany where diesels had been

invented. What's more Perkins had perfected their engines in the light of eight years' operational experience of high production in Peterborough and arduous working conditions in all theatres of the war. The Eastfield factory was used for production while Queen Street continued in use for testing all prototypes and for rebuilding the reconditioned engines.

So great was the post-war demand for Perkins engines that the new up-to-date plant at Eastfield, equipped for mass production on a scale impossible in the old Queen Street works, was by 1947 found to be too small. The optimistic Festival of Britain staged in 1951 saw the Eastfield plant doubled in size to cater for a world busy starting life anew - and a mere three years later it had trebled, and had become a major employer in Peterborough. Back in 1946 the company had employed a workforce of around 700; by 1950 this had become more than 3,000 - and by 1956 Perkins' employees numbered around 6,150! Further expansion followed at regular intervals throughout the 1960s and 70s until the plant reached its present size of 1.8 million square feet on a 122.4-acre site.

Perkins was launched on the London Stock Exchange in July 1951. It was a great success with debenture stock of £1.5 million being fully subscribed immediately.

In 1957 Perkins introduced their bigger and better R6 engine. Designed for the modern trucks that were rolling off the productions lines of the major manufacturers, the new engine packed more punch than the earlier P6.

A partnership of mutual benefit came about in 1959, when the Canadian manufacturers of tractors and combine harvesters Massey-Ferguson made an offer for all F Perkins Ltd's shares. The offer was accepted, Perkins gaining the financial support needed for their further expansion while MF secured an assured supply of engines for their machines.

While all this was being accomplished in Peterborough, major activity was taking place overseas.... Throughout the 1960s exports of over 80 percent of Perkins production had been maintained. Nevertheless there were many countries seeking support in local engine production as their own economies developed - and wherever a country was seen to be actively looking for help, Perkins stepped in to offer license agreements, training, technical support and all the necessary help needed to achieve local production.

Perkins' first overseas out-station had been opened in 1949 in Johannesburg, to cater not only for the potential of the immensely wealthy and productive Union of South Africa but to provide sales and service facilities throughout colonial southern Africa. Business was so good that a South African subsidiary company was formed in the same

Below: *A special engine leaving Peterborough in 1960 with the millionth Perkins engine for export.*

year. From here to Australia was only a week or two's sailing by cargo ship in the days when British merchantmen flying the Red Duster represented the largest cargo carrier in the world. Aircraft then concentrated on the lucrative mail and luxury passenger trade.

Perkins Diesel (Overseas) Propriety Ltd were established, in 1950, on the fringe of Victoria's Dandenong mountain ranges not far from Melbourne, a major sea port, to look after business throughout the Commonwealth of Australia. Sales and services for the entire sub-continent were handled from this point.

Markets closer to home were not neglected as Moteurs Perkins SA was established at St Denis, an industrial suburb of Paris. The highly satisfactory French output was sold to manufacturers of industrial plant, farm machinery and the makers of lorries or 'les camions' to use the French expression for commercial vehicles. French buses of the period, based on pre-war designs, had a character of their own exemplified by a roomy balcony for fresh air minded passengers at the rear.

Perkins' former Indian connection was re-established in 1953 with the conclusion of a manufacturing agreement with a Madras based company, Simpson & Co Ltd. Unlike the previous arrangement by which English vehicles were exported to British India the newly independent Commonwealth country Bharaj (India) was fast becoming a major industrial force in the world. Simpsons built Perkins diesels under licence for sale to Indian makers of lorries and buses, those colourful vehicles whose drivers are inspired by sublime faith in the gods to do mighty deeds on the roads of the sub-continent. The development of civil engineering projects by Indian engineers and architects follows in the best traditions of generations of Britons who planned the railways, docks and water conservation and irrigation works in the days before Perkins engines were invented. Now as elsewhere in the world Perkins diesels provide mobile and efficient power units for such projects.

From one of the world's oldest civilisations to Germany - the home of the inventor of the Diesel engine named after him - was another triumphal step in the remarkable history of Perkins: in 1958 Perkins Motoren GmbH came into being. The establishment of the Perkins sales and service facility at Aschaffenburg has led to it growing into one of the largest of the overseas markets, catering as it does for much of Northern and Central Europe.

In the same year Perkins moved into a Spain which, under the rule of General Franco, was developing its coastal holiday resorts to cater for the sun starved peoples of industrial northern Europe. Spain was not then regarded by the man in the street as an industrial nation in spite of its shipbuilding and motor engineering expertise. Perkins engines proved as popular with Spanish manufacturers who equipped their trucks and tractors with reliable English designed, Madrid built diesel engines.

Another cross oceanic journey by the indomitable Perkins Sales and Development team led to the United States of Brazil where in 1959 Motores Perkins SA dos Brasil was set up in Sao Paulo. Surprisingly Perkins engines were exported from here not only to major US manufacturers of farm and industrial tractors, but even more happily to the great Detroit and Des Moines truck makers in the USA.

This breakthrough was capped in 1960 by Perkins driving a wagon, diesel engined of course, through the protective trade embargoes which isolated American industry from foreign competition. As English car manufacturers were finding the American market difficult to enter for a variety of reasons, mostly aimed at keeping foreign goods out of US markets, this was the most fantastic feather in Perkins cap. The US truck industry of gigantic firms building gargantuan trucks to ferry goods across a colossus of a country fell to Perkins of Peterborough.

Perkins Engines Inc of Wixom, Michigan at the heart of the Great Lakes industrial hinterland, co-ordinated the sale of all Perkins products throughout the USA. The major truck building firms, in a country so large that trucking is one of the major industries with a very powerful political lobby, went overboard to such an extent that Perkins diesels were standard fittings in the best known American made trucks.

Perkins Engines also crossed the international border to cover the very distinct market in Canada, a North American country which is not at all American in the US style.

As Perkins expanded into the Argentine the company history could be read almost as a travellers tale. The settlements lost in the vast distances of this land of pasture and savanna, fringed by mountains in the west and a small string of cities along the east coast, today rely on road transport to fill the gaps in a railway system dwarfed by nature. Perkins Argentina SA

Top: *Perkins employees coming to work through the Covered Way, which was dismantled in the 1980s and is now the site of Sainsury's.*

provided engines for local branches of Ford and Chrysler, all nationalised by the Peron government. The company also won a considerable share of the enormous farm equipment market. This then included over twenty makers of the combine harvesters which relied on Perkins engines as they lumbered across the fertile cornfields of the plains made productive by an amazing racial mix of settlers.

The astounding expansion overseas which Perkins has enjoyed in the last five decades would not have happened but for the skills and dedication of those responsible for the development of the company at home. In a highly competitive world of industrial espionage and copying to the N'th Degree no firm can stand still and survive. Perkins has kept its lead by continuous research and development. The descendants of the fabulous little Ferguson tractor were all equipped with Perkins diesel engines.

The revolutionary Prima high speed direct injection car diesel won the Queen's Award for Technological Achievement to cap four Queen's Awards for Export, justly earned by a firm which exports over 85percent of its products, not to mention those made abroad.
Perkins has a company history which places the firm at the leading edge of British endeavour, a position held by adhering to traditions of excellence when others choose short cuts and fall out.

Today, Perkins is still a major force in Peterborough's industrial scene as well as in the worldwide market place. Many years ago, Frank Perkins adopted a phrase from the Old Testament as his own fundamental principle: 'Where there is no vision, the people perish.' These forceful words were carved above the North office block at Eastfield by way of a tribute to the handling of its successive trials and tribulations. Clearly, Perkins has not only survived but has prospered, and is looking forward into the new millennium with confidence and optimism.

***Top:** North office block at Eastfield. **Below:** An aerial view of Perkins' site during the 1950s.*

Events & occasions

Both pages: Unlucky for some, though not for Watkins and Stafford.... Allocated as number 13 in the Civic Week parade back in 1929, this enormous easy chair *(above)* appears to have won second prize. The unusual float constructed by the local furniture company certainly deserved to come out top in ingenuity and interest value! Large crowds turned out to watch the parade on that pleasant June day, the little ones pushing their way to the front to get a better view, and the chair 'furnished' the watching crowds with something to smile about as it passed them. The children especially would have loved the giant chair that reminded them of Gulliver's travels in Brobdingnag, or Jack's adventures in the land of giants at the top of the beanstalk; this young boy was fascinated enough by the exhibit to pose alongside it for a photograph. Watkins & Stafford took the opportunity to advertise their services as the chair went by, labelling the chair as 'One small item from our huge stock' *(top)*. Many ingenious floats and tableaux took part, each one - like this one entered by A B Gibson Ltd featuring New Zealand butter - *(facing page)* gaily decorated; this is one set of photographs that we would appreciate seeing in colour!

The Civic Week parade was an enormous event. The streets of Peterborough were hung with bunting, flowers and garlands, and Union Jacks hung from every available window. There was much rattling of collecting boxes as the procession made its way along the streets of the city, and spectators were invited to dig deep in their pockets to support the War Memorial Hospital, where a fresh infusion of funds were urgently needed. The hospital, which had opened only the year before, wanted to add a children's wing. The facility had been built as a memorial to those who gave their lives for their country during the first world war. The hospital got its new wing, which later the same year was opened by Prince George.

A glance at the 1940s

HOT OFF THE PRESS

At the end of World War II in 1945 the Allies had their first sight of the unspeakable horrors of the Nazi extermination camps they had only heard of until then. In January, 4,000 emaciated prisoners more dead than alive were liberated by the Russians from Auschwitz in Poland, where three million people, most of them Jews,were murdered. The following year 23 prominent Nazis faced justice at Nuremberg; 12 of them were sentenced to death for crimes against humanity.

THE WORLD AT LARGE

The desert area of Alamogordo in New Mexico was the scene of the first atomic bomb detonation on July 16, 1945. With an explosive power equal to more than 15,000 tons of TNT, the flash could be seen 180 miles away. President Truman judged that the bomb could secure victory over Japan with far less loss of US lives than a conventional invasion, and on 6th August the first of the new weapons was dropped on Hiroshima. Around 80,000 people died.

ROYAL WATCH

By the end of World War II, the 19-year-old Princess Elizabeth and her distant cousin Lieutenant Philip Mountbatten RN were already in love. The King and Queen approved of Elizabeth's choice of husband, though they realised that she was rather young and had not mixed with many other young men. The engagement announcement was postponed until the Princess had spent four months on tour in Africa. The couple's wedding on 20th November 1947 was a glittering occasion - the first royal pageantry since before the war.

The sideshows had been visited, the games played, the competitions won or lost and the rides around the factory grounds enjoyed, and now it was time for the thousands of employees and their families to refresh the 'inner man'. To celebrate the Works and Home day back in 1955, the extension to Perkins Eastfield factory had been crammed with nicely set-out tables and gaily hung with coloured bunting and patriotic Union Jacks that went a long way towards creating

that vital party atmosphere. Crates of soft drinks had been bought in. Huge urns filled to the maximum with water had been boiled for tea and coffee. The caterers had packed thousands of boxes with sandwiches, cakes and whatever else could be fitted inside, and now it was 'all systems go' for a frenzied hour or two. Note the tablecloths, which interestingly have been printed with the company's well-known 'four circles' logo. Though many people have already been served, a queue of people still waits to be given their party food, so these white-coated workers have some way to go yet before they can put their feet up and perhaps find time to snatch a quick cup of tea for themselves. We can't see exactly what the little boy in the foreground is eating, but it looks suspiciously like ice cream. It seems as though at least one person in the queue has grown tired of waiting!

Above: Close examination of this tranquil view of Town Bridge reveals that Bridge Street was decorated with flags and bunting, and crowns were mounted on the lamp standards. This pinpoints the date as June 1953, which saw countrywide celebrations for the Queen's coronation.

The coronation was a red letter day in the diary of everyone in town. Not only were there the official events such as the carnival parade to look forward to, but there were the many street parties, dances and fireworks parties to enjoy. The Queen's coronation was largely responsible for making television popular. Television was still a great novelty at the time, and the coronation ceremony was the very first TV programme that thousands of people had ever seen - a difficult concept for us to grasp so many years on, when we are used to being surrounded by technology of all kinds. But for those who were privileged to be among those early viewers, the sight was one they will never forget.

Many are not aware that the Queen's beautiful coronation dress was itself symbolic, being embroidered with the emblems of the Dominions - India, Canada, New Zealand and Australia. When the ceremony was over, the Queen rode happily back to the palace in her golden coach, wearing the crown and carrying the orb and sceptre.

On a different note, Town Bridge itself - constructed from reinforced concrete - was opened in 1934, replacing the old iron bridge that had stood there for more than 50 years.

Right: We have no date for this photograph, though the flags and garlands point to a time of celebration. The occasion could possibly have been the Civic Week of June 1929, when Peterborough had a number of causes to celebrate. Just a few weeks earlier on 30th April the Mayor, Councillor A E Craig, had started up the steam digger and cut the first sod for Peterborough's new Town Hall, and Prince George laid the foundation stone on 28th June. The Bull is a familiar landmark in this view, and the decorations hung from pole to pole across the street must have made Westgate a riot of colour. Note the vehicle in the right foreground of the picture; at first glance it would appear to be the sidecar of a motor bike, but a closer look identifies it as one of those nippy boat-tail cars that gained a certain following in earlier decades. The vehicle's size and fuel consumption would have worked in its favour, but the boat-tail was surely a cold and draughty motor, and its narrow wire wheels would not have made for good road holding, especially on those cobbled roads. The road itself is worth a second glance. Back then nobody would have thought twice about it, but note the huge expanse of cobbled roadway and imagine the manpower needed to lay those granite setts on every road in the city!

KV
1638

Traffic congestion was becoming a problem in Peterborough by the early 1950s, as can be seen by this view of Bridge Street in 1953 - and on the right of the photograph yet another driver prepares to join the fast-growing number of motorists in the city. At the time of the photograph Peterborough was shifting into party mood ready for the Queen's coronation, and in every street banners, garlands, crowns and thousands of yards of bunting flapped gaily overhead. The Queen was crowned on 2nd June, and that spring was particularly cool; the lady cyclist on the left was well wrapped up against the cold in coat and headscarf. The coolness of the weather was not allowed to spoil the coronation celebrations, however, and street parties and fireworks displays were held across the city to welcome Her Majesty to the throne.
Buses have long been regarded as very handy mobile advertisement hoardings, and the Number 305 Wootton Avenue bus on the left advises motorists and pedestrians alike to use Bovril. Early Bovril slogans were not without a touch of humour ('I hear they want more!' says one nervous bull to another), and their ingenuity made Bovril into a household name. Interestingly, the catchphrase 'Bovril prevents that sinking feeling' was designed before World War I but was withheld at the time as a mark of respect for the families of those lost on the 'Titanic' in 1912.

301
ANGEL HOTEL
RESTAURANT
AEW 523

The coronation of the Queen in 1953 gave everyone a chance to declare their loyalty - and it was party time in Peterborough. Garlands and banners were hung in windows, lines of bunting stretched across every street, and though the weather on the big day was inclined to be cool and rather damp, it didn't stop the children from enjoying their street parties. Perhaps a few of these people caught on camera in Long Causeway, decked out in patriotic red, white and blue for the event, would have been able to watch the ceremony in Westminster Abbey on television; it was the first time the coronation of a British monarch had ever been filmed. Television sets were expensive, however, and though Britain had a television service as early as 1936 (though the service was suspended during World War II), few people could afford to buy them - and the range of programmes was very limited anyway. By the 1950s

sets were beginning to get cheaper, and the Queen's Coronation presented many families with the ideal reason to buy or rent a TV. Those who did not simply crowded into the parlours of more fortunate neighbours to watch the event!
To many, the coronation of Queen Elizabeth II signalled the beginning of a 'new Elizabethan age'; the occasion even called for the writing of new songs; perhaps some readers will remember 'Let's all be new Elizabethans'?

A glance at the 1940s

MELODY MAKERS

The songs of radio personalities such as Bing Crosby and Vera Lynn were whistled, sung and hummed everywhere during the 1940s. The 'forces' sweetheart' brought hope to war-torn Britain with 'When the Lights go on Again', while the popular crooner's 'White Christmas' is still played around Christmas time even today. Who can forget songs like 'People Will Say we're in Love', 'Don't Fence Me In', 'Zip-a-dee-doo-dah', and 'Riders in the Sky'?

INVENTION AND TECHNOLOGY

Inspired by quick-drying printers' ink, in 1945 Hungarian journalist Laszlo Biro developed a ballpoint pen which released viscous ink from its own reservoir as the writer moved the pen across the page. An American inventor was working on a similar idea at the same time, but it was Biro's name that stuck. A few years later Baron Bich developed a low cost version of the pen, and the 'Bic' ballpoint went on sale in France in 1953.

SCIENCE AND DISCOVERY

In 1943 Ukrainian-born biochemist Selman Abraham Waksman made a significant discovery. While studying organisms found in soil he discovered an antibiotic (a name Waksman himself coined) which was later found to be the very first effective treatment for tuberculosis. A major killer for thousands of years, even the writings of the ancient Egyptians contain stories of people suffering from tuberculosis. Waksman's development of streptomycin brought him the 1952 Nobel Prize for Medicine.

These crowds had gathered to hear the opening address that welcomed them to the Perkins' Works and Home day in July 1955, and it would have made interesting listening. They would have heard, for example, that the Royal Navy's X-type five-man midget submarines were to be powered by Perkins engines. Closer to home and of more personal interest was the fact that each of Perkins' employees who earned more than £5 a week would from now on be receiving one of those large white five-pound notes in their pay packets in place of the traditional five one-pound notes, emphasising the growing prosperity of the mid-1950s (not to mention saving the time spent in counting out all those ones!). Some traditions die hard, however, and among them was the way one dressed for a day out.

Best clothes were obviously the order of the day for any special occasion, and hats and ties appear to have been obligatory, at least among the older men and women. Back in the 1950s people did 'dress up' far more than they do today, of course, and even a simple shopping trip called for a change of clothes; casual wear was reserved for the home or the holidays. Looking back, it is difficult to put a date to exactly when general attitudes began to change, but it probably began with the younger generation and changing fashions. Where today we would have seen shorts or trousers, the ladies here have each donned their light summery clothes - those very feminine full skirts that were typical of the day.

Above: *When the Queen was crowned in a Westminster Abbey service on 2nd June 1953, a mere eight years after the end of World War Two, the nation relaxed for the first time and really went to town on the celebrations that welcomed her to the throne. Each town and city, every village institute and church, held their own event, which could range from a simple street party to a big parade. Their joy was tinged with sadness, of course, for the Queen's father, King George VI, was genuinely mourned by the whole nation. Many were in tears when they heard of his death from lung cancer; the King had been a heavy smoker for many years. But his daughter, who had begun her training for the throne early, when Edward VIII's abdication in 1936 made her the heir presumptive to the throne, was already a popular figure, and Peterborough took her to their hearts. The celebrations left few without a precious collection of happy memories to look back on and treasure. Who among those who watched it on TV can forget the sight of the new Queen being anointed with oil and having the crown placed solemnly upon her head?*
The news on the morning of the coronation carried another report that the world had been waiting for - New Zealander Edmund Hillary, with John Hunt and Sherpa Tensing, had reached the summit of Everest. The Daily Express headline said it all: 'All this and Everest Too'!

Shopping spree

Isn't it amazing how familiarity can breed, if not contempt, at least inattention? Passers-by in Midgate were so used to seeing the Swan Inn that they rarely if ever stopped to admire the ancient building, which dated back around 300 years. Back in the 17th century the London coach, the 'Peterborough Diligence', left The Swan at five o'clock in the morning for the long, bumpy ride to Holborn. The old hostelry continued to advertise their 'good stabling' facilities into the 20th century. Sadly, The Swan fell victim to the hungry bulldozer in the 1960s, and it was demolished to make room for the new Hereward Centre. With it went a piece of irreplaceable Peterborough history.

Alongside is a well-stocked (or perhaps we should say over-stocked?) shop, which may or may not be a pawnbroker's. Only one of its golden balls remains of the traditional three; we can only hope that no hapless customer was browsing below when the other two parted company with their chains....
By the 1960s pawnbrokers were largely concentrating on alternative business. It was during the poverty-stricken 1920s and 30s that their services were regularly called upon, when unemployment or poor pay reduced many housewives to putting their husband's only good suit in pawn every Monday morning and redeeming it again at the end of the week so that it could be worn over the weekend.

Right: A scene to bring back memories! Peterborough cattle market, with its noise and bustle, where beasts were discussed, bought and sold by farmers who for many years had made the journey into the city from the outlying areas. The cattle market was running at a loss, however, and though the old facility had been an integral part of the city's life from the time it was opened in 1866, the last beasts were sold there in 1972 and the market closed down.

The sale of sheep and poultry had also been a part of market life, and as December wore on and it neared Christmas, the poultry auctions would have been lively affairs. Chickens and turkeys of all sizes to suit every oven and every family, some oven ready, others not, were offered for sale. Bids were taken and accepted, birds were carried home triumphantly to grace the traditional Christmas table with the accompanying Brussels sprouts, carrots, roast potatoes and chipolata sausages. Makes you hungry just thinking about it, doesn't it? Today the scene is very different, as the general market that had up to 1963 been held in Cathedral Square was moved lock, stock and barrel into new premises built on the site of the old cattle market.

Below: A huge sign prominently placed in the plain view of passers by proudly announced the advent of 'Your Magnificent New Store' as contracted to Bovis, and supported by its framework of scaffolding, Marks & Spencer's store rose block by block to take its place alongside Woolworths in Bridge Street. The proposed opening date was announced as Spring 1964, neatly dating the photograph for us. Marks & Spencer has suffered from an unfortunate 'fuddy-duddy' image in recent years, but the quality of its clothing and the excellence of its food department has never been in doubt, and M & S remains the favourite store with thousands of shoppers, for under and outer wear and food. Marks and Spencer began life in Britain in the early years of the 20th century when Marks' Penny Bazaar opened up in the market in Leeds, West Yorkshire.

The new Peterborough Marks & Spencer replaced the old City Cinema, which had provided Peterborians with entertainment since it was built in 1927. The building also boasted a cafe, and its first floor regularly echoed to the music of the waltz and the slow foxtrot. The high quality sprung dance floor was popular with lovers of ballroom dancing. Peterborough lost the City Cinema in March 1960, and soon after that it was demolished to make room for the new Marks & Spencer store.

A glance at the 1950s

WHAT'S ON?

Television hit Britain in a big way during the 1950s. Older readers will surely remember 'Double Your Money', 'Dixon of Dock Green' and 'Dragnet' (whose characters' names were changed 'to protect the innocent').

Commercial television was introduced on 22nd September 1955, and Gibbs SR toothpaste were drawn out of the hat to become the first advert to be shown. Many believed adverts to be vulgar, however, and audiences were far less than had been hoped for.

GETTING AROUND

The year 1959 saw the development of the world's first practical air-cushion vehicle - better known to us as the hovercraft. The earliest model was only able to travel at slow speeds over very calm water and was unable to carry more than three passengers. The faster and smoother alternative to the sea ferry quickly caught on, and by the 1970s a 170-ton car-carrying hovercraft service had been introduced across the English Channel.

SPORTING CHANCE

The four-minute mile had remained the record since 1945, and had become regarded as virtually unbreakable. On 6th May 1954, however, Oxford University student Roger Bannister literally ran away with the record, accomplishing the seemingly impossible in three minutes 59.4 seconds. Bannister collapsed at the end of his last amazing lap, even temporarily losing his vision. By the end of the day, however, he had recovered sufficiently to celebrate his achievement in a London night club!

How many readers remember having a cup of coffee or afternoon tea in the Home Made Cake Cafe in Church Street? The fact that you could eat 'luncheon' there was advertised on the sign above the door of this rather smart establishment, taking us back to the days before you snatched a quick cuppa or queued for fries in a cardboard carton at one of the city's burger bars. A mother has left her pram outside while she pops in for a little refreshment; was the baby still inside it? We would

not think of parking our children outside shops today, but somehow those long-ago days seemed less dangerous in every way. A ham and salad sandwich made with Hovis was no doubt on the menu, and behind the name of the popular bread lies an interesting story. When the loaf was first produced, the makers ran a competition to decide on a suitably snappy name for the bread. The winner (whose name has been lost in the mists of time) came up with 'Hovis' - a contraction of the Latin 'hominus vis', meaning 'the strength of man'. Adjoining the cafe were Drydens on one side and W & J Brown, florist and seedsman, on the other, where you could purchase seeds and every other accessory so important to gardeners across the city. And if you were not among the 'grow it yourself' enthusiasts you could, of course, buy yourself a bunch of the finished product to take home.

Traditionally customers queued to be served - a far cry from today's plastic packs!

There was a time when small butchers such as Huntings in Bridge Street were a common sight around Peterborough. Sadly, many of them are gone, together with the personal service we once took for granted. Small grocery chains and corner butchers were the traditional way to shop, and customers would queue to be served while the butcher cubed our stewing steak and cut our sausages from a long string hanging over the counter. A far cry from today's plastic packs! People might have had to wait a while longer to be served, but at least they had the benefit of personal attention from the staff. Things were to remain that way until the mid-1950s, when self-service shopping began to catch on. The trend started slowly, but it was the thin end of the wedge. At the time of the photograph, Huntings' shop was advertised for sale, and the date of the sale reveals that the year was 1963, by which time self service shopping would have just begun to make its presence felt. Over the last forty or so years there has been a shift towards super- and hyper-markets and out of town shopping.

On a different note, the number of cycles standing against the kerb or propped up by the wall reminds us of the days when we didn't all own a family car - and also brings to mind the gentler days when we could leave a cycle outside a shop and expect to find it still there on our return!

Below: What a pity that we can't get close enough to peer into Pearson's window and see exactly what was on offer, and what the prices were! They are tempting none of these passers-by in off the street, however, and the thoughts of these people are clearly on other things. We might hazard a guess that the photograph was taken early in the year, as although warm coats and hats are in evidence, gardening implements and seeds are being displayed here.

As far as we can see, Pearsons occupied three properties in Lincoln Road, Millfield, and the shop seems to have been the kind of place where you could buy anything from lamps and trays to larger items of furniture. A couple of carpets and a chair stand on the wide pavement outside to tempt punters to buy, while that indispensable piece of 1960s occasional furniture, a leather pouffe, adds its own kind of charm to the display. The gardening and hardware department further along is also taking advantage of the dry weather to display his wheelbarrow, lawn mower and rack of packets of seeds. We note that the wheelbarrow is not one of James Dyson's innovative ballbarrows, and close inspection reveals that the lawn mower alongside it is of the push-pull persuasion, one of the kind that was unaided by petrol or electricity and depended on muscular arms. Long live the Flymo....

Bottom: Remember Tuf shoes? The popular brand of stout footwear was sold at this shop in Midgate, along with a thousand and one other items. Duffle coats, trousers, jackets, shirts, boots, you name it - if it was workwear - and you could almost certainly buy it here. Stuffed to bursting point with an immense range of goods, this was the obvious port of call for any bloke who needed either working gear or casual clothes. During the 1960s most children and many adults, both men and women, wore a duffle coat; those big toggles were easy for little fingers (and big ones too) to manage, and the hood kept their ears warm in the chilly winds of winter. Denim jeans had already become entrenched as the fashion of the decade - though they were in fact to remain popular right up to the end of the 1990s. Denim jeans were first introduced last century, when a factory in Nimes in France produced them as heavy duty workwear. Levi Strauss began to make jeans in the late nineteenth century, mostly for the gold mining industry. They added the now-familiar rivets as reinforcements to stop the weight of the gold nuggets tearing the pockets.

By 1998 younger people were beginning to turn away from denim, especially as their elders (not to mention a number of prominent political figures!) were still wearing their jeans. Far be it from the average teenager to be seen in public wearing clothes that in any way resembled their parents' - and jeans began to lose their popularity.

A scene to bring memories flooding back - Peterborough Market in its traditional position in Cathedral Square, and many readers will remember with fondness the hours they spent browsing among the many stalls on market days. Peterborians, who love a bargain as much as the next person, would have made a beeline for this spot in the old days. The market was busy when the photographer captured this view for posterity, a bustling scene, full of life and with a character of its very own. The day was obviously a cool one judging by the number of ladies among the shoppers wearing headscarves.

During the 1950s older ladies usually favoured a neat little hat, while the younger women still opted to wear the very practical headscarf, that could be folded away in a pocket or handbag, and brought out in wind or rain. These ladies were in good company - Her Majesty has long been a keen wearer of headscarves. Note, too, the pram pushed by one of the young women; those lovely coach built prams were a thing of beauty - but what a lot of space they took up in the average hallway or living room! Today's buggies might not be in the same league as the old prams, but they are far more practical.

Above: One up on your average Boots store! This 'medieval' Boots is not as old as it would first appear, however, as it was built comparatively recently, in 1911. Though only imitation, its half-timbered frontage is nevertheless a talking point, closely linking the building to the history of the city. Statues of five historical figures are mounted on the front of the building, painted in the medieval style. Centrally placed is King Henry VIII; Aethelwold, Bishop of Winchester and the Saxon King Peada find a place at second floor level, while below them stand Prince Rupert of the Rhine, a Royalist commander in the Civil War (and the beheaded King Charles I's nephew), and on the opposite side of the building his old enemy Robert Devereux, one of Cromwell's commanders. All long gone from this life, though the building that commemorates them lives on as a branch of Burger King.
The cars parked along the kerbside and the knee-length fashions in Paige's window point to the mid to late 1960s as the probably date of this photograph. How many of our readers would admit to driving a Morris 1100 in their younger days? (And how many of them had to replace the rear sub-frame at some point?) Interestingly, there is not a yellow line in sight along the kerb, though parking would probably have been restricted.

Right: Another busy day for market traders and shoppers alike, and many Peterborians will remember this flower stall and its cheerful containers of daffodils and tulips (or carnations and chrysanthemums, according to the time of year). Flowers have always been one of the most popular gifts to show one's love and appreciation. How many young men will have bought roses for their wives or girl friends, or girls added a bunch or two of daffs to their shopping baskets to take home to Mum? It is many years now since we were able to visit the market in Cathedral Square, or, for that matter, see the Gates Memorial in all its glory, and this reminder of the way things used to be will bring back many fond memories.
Even in ancient times Cathedral Square was at the heart of the city's life, and markets, fairs, meetings and ceremonies have traditionally been held there. Less pleasant for some, the stocks and pillory would more than likely have also stood there, and those unfortunates sentenced to a few hours' punishment - deserved or not - would suffer the taunts (and possibly the odd bad egg or two) of the market shoppers. To them, it was all part of the day's entertainment, though perhaps not so entertaining to the poor souls who were on the receiving end!

PRUDENTIAL
BUILDING SOCIETY
True-Form
PURDYS
RADIO
TRADE & GENERAL INTEREST
TOWN HALL
SEPT 25-28

It really takes you back, doesn't it? Can't you just feel the atmosphere of the old open market? The typical open wicker shopping basket, the scarves and little hats of the older ladies, the hairstyles of the younger ones, and the just-below-the-knee hemlines identify the date of this photograph as the early 1960s (hemlines were rising, though, and the real mini-skirts lay just around the corner). The days of this open market were numbered, however, when this nostalgic scene was captured, as the new facility was opened in 1963.
The well-stocked fruit stall in the photograph would have made a good starting place for a lot of Peterborian housewives, who week after week would catch a bus into town and tour the market to find the best - and cheapest - apples, pears, oranges, grapefruit and bananas. Buying potatoes and tomatoes from one stall,

apples and sprouts from another and perhaps cabbage and a couple of grapefruit from a third have always been part of the fun of bargain hunting in the market. The prices charged by markets and street traders have traditionally been a few coppers cheaper than the average high street greengrocer would charge, and a weekly walk around the market could save a shilling or two here and there, and stretch the inadequate housekeeping money a little bit further.

A glance at the 1950s

MELODY MAKERS

Few teenage girls could resist the blatant sex-appeal of 'Elvis the Pelvis', though their parents were scandalised at the moody Presley's provocatively gyrating hips. The singer took America and Britain by storm with such hits as 'Jailhouse Rock', 'All Shook Up' and 'Blue Suede Shoes'. The rhythms of Bill Haley and his Comets, Buddy Holly, Chuck Berry, and Roy Orbison (who had a phenomenal three-octave voice) turned the 1950s into the Rock 'n' Roll years.

INVENTION AND TECHNOLOGY

Until the late 1950s you did not carry radios around with you. Radios were listened to at home, plugged into a mains socket in every average sitting room. Japan was in the forefront of electronic developments even then, and in 1957 the Japanese company Sony introduced the world's very first all-transistor radio - an item of new technology that was small enough to fit into your pocket. The major consumer product caught on fast - particularly with teenage listeners.

SCIENCE AND DISCOVERY

DNA (deoxyribonucleic acid) was first defined as long ago as 1953, and the effects have been far-reaching. The key discovery was developed over the following years and today DNA fingerprinting has become an accepted part of life. Genetic diseases such as hemophilia and cystic fibrosis have been identified. Criminals are continually detected and brought to justice. Biological drugs have been developed. More controversially, drought and disease-resistant plants have been engineered - and Dolly the sheep has been produced.

At leisure

Below: Was this Peterborough fire engine the best exhibit of the day at Perkins' Works and Home exhibition back in 1955? These children obviously thought it was, and they swarmed all over the engine under the watchful eye of a bewildered fire fighter (who even if he was a father had probably never before had so many children to take care of all at the same time!)

The kids, however, would have meant no harm back in those gentler days of the 1950s, when there was very little vandalism, and children still respected parents, teachers, the local bobby and the irate neighbour who was rapidly growing sick of being asked 'Can we have our ball back, Mister?'

These children would have explored every inch of the exciting vehicle, pulling and pushing every button and lever, poking and prodding the engine's every nook and cranny, and trying to unroll its length of hose. Being allowed to ring the bell would have been the day's crowning glory to every one of these children, boys and girls alike - though those were the days before women fire fighters were an accepted part of the force. How many of these kids went home at the end of the day saying 'I want to be a fireman when I grow up, Dad'?

The Lincoln was made by Ford in America and assembled in Britain

Has the owner of this lovely left hand drive Lincoln decided to relax for an hour or two and spend the afternoon at the pictures? 'Roman Holiday', new to our screens in 1953 and billed as 'The gayest film of the year', was being shown at the Odeon at the time, so if this driver was an old romantic at heart he would have been in for a treat. The film's plot followed the old 'rich falls for poor' story line (which nevertheless still seems to work), and a princess's official visit to Rome forms the background to the charming and funny film. The princess manages to slip away incognito, meets up with a good looking newspaper man - and the inevitable, of course, happens. The film's atmosphere is perfect; skies of cloudless blue, hot sunshine, the shady gardens of the Roman forum, the fabulous Coliseum and the glamorous streets of Rome provide the perfect setting for two people to fall in love, and Audrey Hepburn and Gregory Peck are memorable as the princess and the reporter in this old-fashioned romance. The superb Lincoln would have been an unusual sight in the streets of Peterborough. Made in America by Ford and assembled in Britain, this family sedan was a rather upmarket motor. Its large chrome grill and white walled tyres mark the design as American, though the Lincoln was small by US standards. Eventually the Ford Consul was to ape the style, though the Consul was smaller to suit British taste.

Above: All aboard for the Continental Express! This was Saturday 9th July 1955, and Perkins were holding their Works and Home day. Out had come the ladders and the decorations, and the factory was gaily hung with colourful bunting and streamers. It was time for employees and their children to have some fun. This beautifully scaled-down loco was one of the most popular attractions on site, and the young driver carefully adjusting one of his rear view mirrors *(bottom)* was definitely taking his job seriously. The speed limit for all vehicles in the yard was on the wall in plain sight nearby - ten miles per hour - but even if the Continental Express was capable of greater speeds, this driver was not going to break the rules. Hundreds of his mates would have given their eye teeth for the opportunity to drive the train, and he was not going to take his responsibility lightly. Responsibility was far from the minds of his passengers, however, and their only interest was in having a good time - and waving to the camera as the photographer snapped them as they were driven by! The miniature railway was an enormously popular attraction, and was probably described by its passengers as 'super-duper'; today of course it would be 'cool' or even 'wicked', especially if you were lucky enough to be the driver - but however it was described, the little train was still reckoned to be great fun. All very thrilling stuff, and calculated to send any child home tired and satisfied at the end of a wonderful day out.

Right: The services of an elephant with a difference were called upon to carry load after load of children around Perkins' factory. His name, we presume, would have been Jumbo, and his keeper would have had little trouble keeping him in order. A simple on/off switch was probably all there was to this wonderful mechanical beast! The queues for this particular ride would have been long, as the elephant was as popular as if he had been of the flesh and blood variety, borrowed for the day from the zoo. Though he wore his head-dress with pride and still had his satisfyingly long trunk and his full complement of tusks, Jumbo had obviously seen better days, his wrinkled legs reminding us of Norah Batty, and his white stuffing peeping sadly out through the numerous tears in his fabric. The children, however, had probably not even noticed any of Jumbo's shortcomings. They couldn't have cared less if he was falling to pieces - they loved him just the same! Perhaps some of these children waving enthusiastically to the photographer will be among those reading this book? More than 40 years may have passed since Jumbo proudly carried them around the factory yard, but they will surely remember him with fondness!

You may or may not believe in UFOs - but flying saucers were definitely to be seen in Peterborough at the 1957 Sports and Family day, when the kids, all children of the company's employees, had a 'smashing' time at the crockery shy.
This young boy's 'flick of the wrist' (with china cups, saucers and plates in place of coconuts) is attracting enormous interest from the crowd, who are watching his accuracy (or otherwise!) with close attention. We have to wonder just how much crockery remained at the end of the day, as this sideshow was obviously enjoying enormous popularity. All the boy's friends are dying to have a go, as, perhaps, was his dad, though the grown ups have absolutely no chance to

get a look in at this particular game. The appeal of the pleasing crash of broken china (and china broken legitimately at that) had too great a pull with the kids!
This marvellous scene is a real study of human character - can't you see intense expectation and interest on virtually every face as they cheer the boy on and wait for the next satisfying smash?

A glance at the 1950s

HOT OFF THE PRESS

The 1950s seemed to be the heyday of spies, and in 1951 the activities of Guy Burgess and Donald Maclean caused a sensation in the country. Both had occupied prominent positions in the Foreign Office, while Burgess had also been a member of MI-6. Recruited by the Russians while at Cambridge University in the 1930s, the traitors provided the Soviets with a huge amount of valuable information. They disappeared in 1951, surfacing in Moscow five years later.

THE WORLD AT LARGE

Plans to develop the economies of member states into one common market came to fruition on 1st January 1958, when the EEC came into operation. The original members were France, Belgium, Luxembourg, The Netherlands, Italy, and West Germany. The Community became highly successful, achieving increased trade and prosperity across Western Europe while at the same time alleviating fear of war which lingered on after the end of World War II. Britain became a member in 1973.

ROYAL WATCH

King George VI's health had been causing problems since 1948, when he developed thrombosis. In 1951 the King - always a heavy smoker - became ill again, and was eventually found to be suffering from lung cancer. His left lung was removed in September of 1951. In January 1952 he waved Princess Elizabeth and Prince Philip off on their tour of Africa; they were never to see him again. The King died on 5th February 1952.

Left: Can't you almost hear the 'Ooh's' and 'Ah's' of pure delight as this group of children (and their mums and dads!) breathlessly watch this high level performance? Apart from the fact that this 'aerial act' was staged at Perkins' Sports and Family Day in June 1952, we have no further information, so we can only imagine the mind-boggling feat that was being performed high above the ground! Was this one of those very funny acts put on by clowns playing pranks on each other and keeping their audience below roaring with laughter? Or was it a high wire act that made them hold their breath anxiously, as a man dressed in spangled tights attempted to ride a monocycle from one side of the wire to the other while juggling with four coloured clubs? (Do you think he's going to fall off, Dad?) Or could it perhaps be a team of trapeze artists in colourful costumes that kept this audience spellbound, hoping against hope that they would not miss the outstretched hands of their partners? Unless one of these children, now grown up and with children and grandchildren of their own, recognises him- or herself among our readers and can remember that wonderful day so many years ago....

Below: 'I want my mum!' sobs this unhappy four-year-old who had become separated from his family during the Sports and Family day held by Perkins back in June 1957. His mother, too, we can imagine, would be terribly upset and searching for him everywhere with very little chance of finding him in the milling crowds, blaming herself for taking her eyes off him for a couple of seconds. But haven't we all been through the same thing? All of us have lost our child at some time or other, or have been on the receiving end of the problem when we were children ourselves! Either way, we can sympathise with both the little boy and his mother. Help was not far away for the little chap, though, as some kind grown up had obviously found him crying and had escorted him to the centre of operations where Mr Tom Parish took the boy under his wing. Mr Parish was the official announcer for the occasion - and this particular announcement would have brought the child's mother running hotfoot to the tent to scold him for wandering off while at the same time she hugged him in relief. For Mr Parish himself, comforting lost children was all part of the day's work....

The Bull Hotel has long been part of Peterborough's history, and dates from the 18th century, when it was a coaching inn. The arched entrance to the old stables, which were situated behind the building, can still be seen today. Since those early days The Bull has seen considerable changes, with a second storey and 22 extra bedrooms built in the early 20th century, and extensions added in the late 1920s. This 1960s photograph reminds us that 30-odd years ago The Bull was advertising itself as the 'finest grill room and restaurant in the city'. The popular hotel was registered with both the AA and the RAC, and a quick glance at the RAC Guide and Handbook for 1967-68 reveals that back in the late 1960s The Bull (which rated two stars at the time) had 82 bedrooms, and bed and breakfast would set you back around 39/6d (just short of £2); evening dinner cost from 12/6d (about 63p). Sounds a snip, doesn't it? Until, that is, you compared it with the average weekly wage at the time.... Today the hotel - a very smart establishment that has earned five-crown standing - is still a popular place with diners, both visitors and local, and boasts a total of 103 bedrooms.

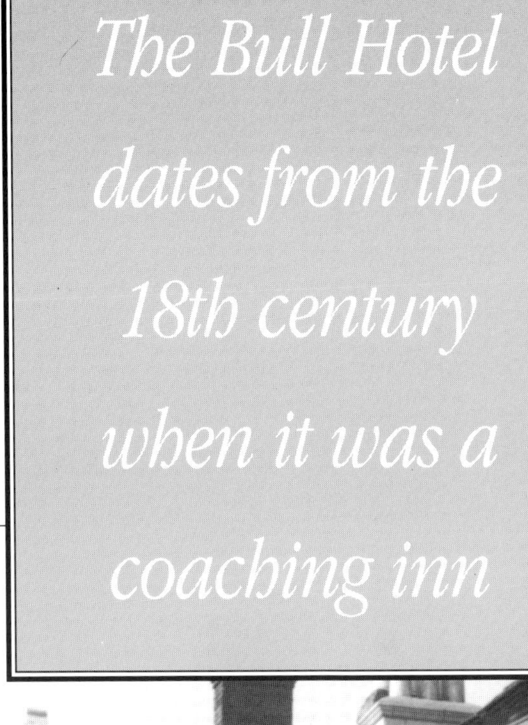

At work

What was it like for the local residents in Henson Street and the surrounding area, to live in the shadow of the enormous gas holders that provided Peterborough with its vital power? We can assume that they - and the odour that tended to hang around them - were simply a fact of life, and that people would have been so used to seeing this or a similar view every time they looked out of their window that they would never give it a second thought. Children certainly grew up in these streets never having known anything else.

The power of gas was discovered back in the late 18th century, and by 1820 gas making was a boom industry, using thousands of tons of coal every year. At that time nearly all the gas was used for lighting rather than for cooking and heating. By the end of the 19th century, however, most of Peterborough's industry was gas powered and gas lamps lit our streets. When gas lamps were first introduced their light seemed so bright that it was compared to daylight, but gas lighting was put well and truly in the shade when the city's first electricity generator was built in 1900.

It was when the Gas Board began to tap supplies from under the North Sea that natural gas took over from town gas, and a number of Peterborough's gas holders were demolished. Some of our readers will know whether this particular one survives or not!

The end of a hard day's work, and these workers at the Perkins factory were as anxious to get home as the next person. Some would have their bikes, others their cars. Many more would be taking the bus, however, for this was 1951 and few ordinary families had their own car at the time. During the 1950s the majority of Britons still held on to their traditions, and men were widely regarded as the bread winners, going out to work every day to keep their wives and families, while their women folk saw to the children, shopped for food at the local shops, made the meals, cleaned the house, and washed and ironed the family's clothes. The second world war changed the way of life for hundreds of men and women, turning generations of tradition upside down. When Britain's men were called into military service, women found themselves doing jobs they had never done before, doing 'jobs for the boys' in positions across the board from engineering works to public transport. Perkins set on their first female shop floor workers in 1940.

In 1951, the Festival of Britain kicked off the new decade, infusing the country with a spirit of new hope and faith in the future. Perkins played their part in the nation-wide event - their engines were exhibited in London, where the cigar-like Skylon, a breathtaking 300-foot high structure, formed part of the Exhibition; illuminated at night, the Skylon was visible for miles around. The nearby Dome of Discovery was a visible sign of national achievement.

There are many who would today count themselves Peterborians whose early years were spent in London, or whose parents moved to the city from London in the late 1960s. The concept of 'new towns' had been discussed and planned since the end of World War II in 1945, with Lord Reith heading up the New Towns Committee. Peterborough formed part of his plans, and preparations were made to more than double the size of the population by the end of the 1980s. In 1969 the city had 81,000 inhabitants, and the original plans were to increase this to 180,000, though this figure was later reduced to 160,000.

The milkman went so far as to leave milk and butter on the doorstep of every new resident

To his credit, Lord Reith realised the importance of different income groups, with both manual and white collar workers. Social life should also be catered for, he argued, with adequate provision in the city for dancing and music, theatre and the arts, shops and churches. New estates of housing of all kinds were built, and the newcomers arrived in Peterborough to an unexpected welcome. Local traders, community workers and neighbours adopted a deliberate policy of making them feel at home, and, so the story goes, the milkmen went so far as to leave three bottles of milk and a pound of butter on the doorsteps of the new residents on their first day in Peterborough.

The photograph was taken in St John's Street in the early 1960s, when St Mary's Court flats were being constructed.

Housing and care for more than 30 years

Axiom Housing Association was founded in 1967 and registered as a Friendly Society moving to Peterborough in 1972. New legislation in the form of the 1974 Housing Act gave Axiom and other similar housing associations access to grant aid to provide rented accommodation and rapid growth followed with 40 homes in management by the end of 1976 and a further 450 in varying stages of planning and development.

Over the next few years many more homes were provided with the Association reaching the milestone of providing its thousandth home in 1985. By this time the accommodation provided covered not only homes for families but also single working people, the elderly and people with special needs all of whom had been in need of help to solve their accommodation difficulties

In 1988 a new Housing Act was passed which enabled housing associations to borrow private finance to add to the reduced amount of public grant available which gave a renewed impetus to the growth of Axiom. In fact the Association's first private borrowing followed in 1989 when, following a ballot, 144 former Development Corporation dwellings were purchased in the Bretton and Ravensthorpe areas of the City.

Since 1989 the Association has raised over £10 million adding this to grants to fund the provision of a further 700 properties in Peterborough and the surrounding areas. As in the early days of the Association the homes are provided to meet a wide range of needs and a feature of recent years has been the development of specialist accommodation in partnership with various voluntary bodies to provide independent living for people who would otherwise be unable to live in their own home.

The Association's original aim was to provide good quality rented accommodation charging rents that were affordable by those who needed homes, and this continues today with the Association's rents being the lowest of any housing association in Peterborough.

Top right: *Ethelred Close.* ***Above:*** *Carl Hall Court, opened in 1985.* ***Below:*** *The opening of Bretton in 1979. Ron Scoffins, Managing Director of Netherton Building Ltd, hands the key to Pat Preston, Chair of the Housing Sub-Committee.*

Successful property marketing the Sharman Quinney way

Take a drive through any part of Peterborough or surrounding towns and villages in the region and you will bear witness to one of the most remarkable local business success stories of the decade.

Back in 1989 amidst the doom and gloom of an economic recession, partners Mike Sharman and Steve Quinney shared a vision on the future of the property market. Customer Service, a phrase that has become an integral part of the English language was in eighties Estate Agency at least, more of an afterthought far less a priority. Messrs Sharman and Quinney had both scaled the heights of the Estate Agency corporate ladder and they realised the way forward for successful property marketing was to introduce an Estate Agency operation with a modern sales-driven concept based on traditional values of Customer Service.

They were to challenge and change Estate Agency attitudes by creating a successful independent Estate Agent - a company owned, operated and effectively managed by Estate Agents rather than banks, building societies or insurance companies as was the case at the time.

With little financial support, the two men decided to swap comfortable lifestyles for the risk of the unknown. Few, if any, believed that 1989 was the right time to start a new business, never mind an Estate Agency business. The post-boom property market was in a recession resulting in a total lack of buyer confidence and property sales at an all-time low. But Sharman and Quinney had the qualities of true pioneers - unswerving belief and confidence in their own ability, a workaholic passion and drive for quality in their chosen industry and most important of all, "fire in the belly".

Above: *Partners Mike Sharman (seated) and Steve Quinney.*

So on October 21st 1989 the company that has come to dominate the property market for so long in this area was born.

Shunning Peterborough's "Estate Agent Alley" in Cowgate, Sharman Quinney was launched from an office in Broadway, Peterborough. Whilst the choice of location may appear insignificant it is typical of the style of leadership from the two entrepreneurs - ignore the competition, be individual and build motivated teams with commitment to service and results. Above all, be successful.

As other companies closed with regularity, Sharman Quinney set about success and growth through market share. The partners inspired and led by example and their individual hands-on management style worked. It didn't take long for word to spread around the Cathedral City that there was a new Estate Agent with a unique and different approach rebelling against the unwritten laws of local Estate Agency and changing the way the industry operated.

Hard work, commitment to service and more hard work combined with unequalled sales results meant that Sharman Quinney boards, especially Sharman Quinney Sold boards, were going up everywhere.

After just four months, the Estate Agent rebels had become market leaders.

Mike Sharman takes up the story: "For years people who should have been treated as valuable potential customers were dictated to by an industry that was complacent. Estate Agency is a service industry and must be customer driven. From day one we broke the rules on business hours by opening seven days a week and staying open until 8pm - often later - during the week. It was obvious that as most Estate Agents at the time worked nine to five, to provide an improved service convenient to the customer we had to be available far beyond these hours." Whilst many of the competition were reluctant to adopt longer opening hours the Sharman Quinney work ethic captured the respect of the public and commanded the local market place.

Within the first twelve months trading the company had already become not only Peterborough's busiest Estate Agency but also one of the busiest in the entire country. Sharman Quinney, the dream of two ambitious and highly motivated businessmen, had turned into an impressive reality and the sign of things to come was evident.

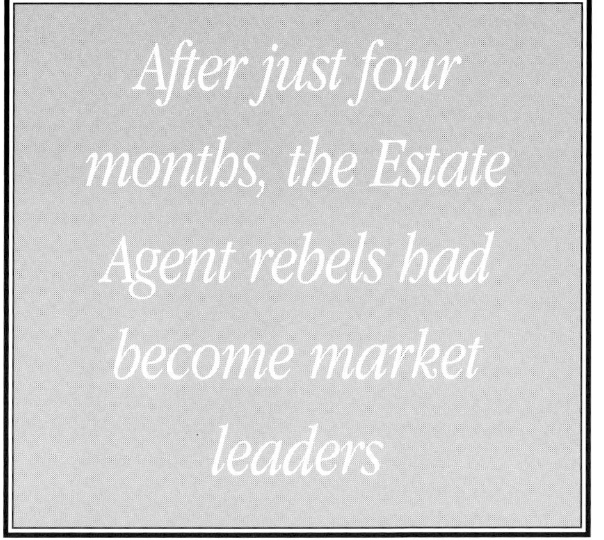

Steve Quinney recalled the scene of a decade ago: "We were new, in terms of our company name, and very different. Our enthusiasm and positive attitude was a breath of fresh air in the property market at the time. We enjoyed the opportunity and challenge, the team spirit and buzz in the office was, as it is today, unreal. We recognised that marketing property need not be complicated although it has become more sophisticated. People buy from people whether it is a product or service and 'buying' the Estate Agency service is no different. Naturally we wanted customers to be on our side and we knew that as long as they could trust us to do the job for them thoroughly, effectively and professionally then our relationship with the customer would work.

"Not only that, word soon got around how hard our company was working. Referrals and recommendations became first the foundation and then the springboard for further success. People would pass by our office at 9.00 and 10.OOpm to see us still on the telephone, still selling property. The fact we were visibly

Below: *The volume of business dictated that the Peterborough Sales headquarters be moved to a high-profile City Centre building in August 1996.*

still working our socks off, and enjoying every minute of it, did us no harm whatsoever."

As Sharman Quinney became increasingly successful and developed a reputation for providing a quality results orientated service the partners decided the time was right to expand the company and opened their second office in 1991, in Yaxley. This led the way for further new office openings in Market Deeping, Ramsey, Whittlesey, Bourne, Oakham, Spalding, Oundle and the market town of Stamford.

The commercial strategy of this ten office strong regional network ensures the company is closely linked and controlled, provides maximum geographical coverage and offers the advantage of the largest database of buyers in the area.

Mike Sharman again, "Each of our outlets conduct business the Sharman Quinney way with the extra benefit of local autonomy and flexibility. We have always been highly selective in our recruitment and employ only those who are driven by the challenge of customer service. Around 80percent of our existing staff were new to Estate Agency and that's always been a deliberate policy. We put a great emphasis on staff training and development, investing time and resources with ongoing training programmes ranging from personal coaching to specialist group training. It is our intention to employ the best Estate Agents in the industry - our responsibility is to help them maximise their potential. Each office has high levels of expectation in terms of performance and results and every office reflects an identical proactive, dynamic attitude towards successful property marketing."

The late nineties will be viewed by the Partners as a time of continuing change. As the multi-million pound business has grown so have individual roles and responsibilities. Lifestyles, career paths and futures have been created with staff numbers now over the one hundred mark.

Top left: *Dawn Webb, now Group Secretary, was a member of the team who joined from day one.*
Right: *Another one sold! A familiar sign of success.*

Steve Quinney concluded "I feel we have remained true to our beliefs and are justifiably proud of our achievements so far. Sharman Quinney are market leaders and the largest Estate Agency and Financial Services network in the region. We aim to create an enjoyable working environment geared towards success, for example we have an Awards Night every year with trophy presentations to provide incentive and opportunities for recognition.

"We have focused on our core business and have developed Sharman Quinney Financial Services into one of the largest introducers of Mortgage and Financial Services business in this part of the country. Sharman Quinney Surveyors comprises of our own team of qualified Chartered Surveyors, with Sharman Quinney New Homes and Sharman Quinney Regional further specialist Estate Agency related services."

The company enjoyed a re-branding in 1998 giving it a more sophisticated up to date image and their offices have seen their share of the premium priced property market rise accordingly.

"With these and many other developments we have been able to promote a number of our Managers to Equity Partner status offering them further incentive, responsibility and authority to help run their local business."

So, never a company to let the grass grow under their feet, what's next for Sharman Quinney?
"We have additional new services and offices to launch that will continue to increase the size of the company and more importantly, provide greater benefit to our customers. And of course we will continually strive for the perfect Estate Agency service wherever our customers needs and expectations take us."

Ten years on and the basics remain the same: high standards of service and success, high levels of expectation and lots of hard work.

The company mission statement serves as a constant reminder -

"To consistently achieve success and excellence in all aspects of Estate Agency and Customer Service." - Sharman Quinney.

Right: *Mark Faulkner the first local Equity Partner who joined the company in 1990.*

Queensgate, the regional shopping centre

The heart of the old cathedral city and market town of Peterborough has been transformed into the shopping capital of the borderlands of the East Midlands and East Anglia. The Queensgate Shopping Centre is unusual in that it has been designed to complement the existing streets and shops of the town centre rather than destroy them.

The design philosophy of the Peterborough Development Corporation was to conserve the old while blending the new with the spirit of the city. Visitors and locals can see for themselves how this has been achieved by an enterprise which won the 1983 Award granted by no less a body than the European International Council of Shopping Centres.

The predominant aim was to increase shop floor space in the fast growing city by 50percent to cater not only for the town but for the region with a population of 600,000 within a twenty mile radius. Some who praise the protected all weather shopping facilities feel that the centre looks in upon itself and shuts out the older shops in existing streets so that there is an invisible barrier through which shoppers must pass. The handsomely finished shop fascias in modern materials reflect the quality of the marble floors of the indoor streets. These like The Rows in Chester are on two floors giving shoppers the opportunity to look up and down in the spacious, well lit, plant filled atria.

The names of the store tenants reflect the aim of such shopping centres which according to a recent international conference is 'to improve the quality of life of customers profitably'. Well, we are a nation of shopkeepers after all and shopping patterns are changing as mature people reclaim their share of the market from the young who dominated it for so long. Queensgate shops now claim that shoppers seek quality and value for their money rather than cheap mass produced throw away items.

Queensgate follows the North American pattern in renting space to outlets other than those catering for the basic daily needs of the average family. These are all located in an exciting environment of interest and colour softened by garden like features and tinkling fountains. Customers can float effortlessly from floor to floor riding upon escalators as they seek the shops they require. The major tenants are easy to find as they enjoy favourable positions near entrances, cafes and open spaces.

Top: *An impression by artist Ann Jasper of the bustling Roman town of Durobrivae.*
Below: *Building work well under way in 1978.*

Shoppers with physical disabilities are provided with a choice of manual or electric wheel chairs and lifts to ease their shopping experience both within the centre and in the surrounding streets. This is a welcome facility for those to whom shop entrance steps form a major barrier. Just as important to all shoppers are the convenient physical links between Queensgate and either easily accessible and affordable car parks or the public transport services which we are exhorted to support. The latter are enhanced by the bus station, with a throughput of 900 buses a day, and a foot bridge to the railway station.

The whole magnificent concept was built by John Laing and funded by Norwich Union. The Queensgate Centre accounts for a third of shopping space in the city centre providing access to and from pedestrianised Church Street, Long Causeway and Bridge Street. Over 2,000 jobs have been provided by the tenants of the Centre in shops ranging from Art shops to travel goods stores.

Ladies can enjoy the attentions of qualified beauticians and then following a meal with friends can shop for jewellery, clothing and shoes. Men about town can outfit themselves for any activity, buy flowers for the women in their lives, visit the bank and buy a book while waiting. Families can add to their musical collections, buy toys for the kids and obtain everything they need to embellish the home.

Queensgate reflects the success of the city for which it was built and has become a show place of Shopping for the Millennium. It exemplifies pleasant comfortable air conditioned shopping as opposed to braving wet and windy or hot and dusty streets in the ultimate shopping experience.

Top left: *Shoppers enjoy the sunshine in the pedestrian precinct.* ***Top right:*** *An interior view of the Queensgate Shopping Centre.* ***Below:*** *An aerial view over Peterborough showing the expanse of the Queensgate Shopping Centre.*

Building on the success of previous generations

Even as a little boy, the founder Robert George Carter knew what he wanted to be when he grew up - he wanted to be a carpenter, like his grandfather. And this was the first of many wise decisions which have led to the R G Carter Group becoming the successful, well-respected construction company that it is today.

Young George, as he chose to be called (George was his grandfather's name) became a carpenter's apprentice at the age of 14, practising his new skills with the tools he had inherited from his grandfather. After his apprenticeship he tried life in London, decided it was not for him, and returned to East Anglia, where he spent the next few years working alongside experienced craftsmen who displayed the high level of skill that was to become so important to George.

In 1914 George Carter joined up and served in France. His bravery, which almost cost him his life on a number of occasions, earned him the Military Medal and the Croix de Guerre. Within three days of being demobbed he found employment on a building site in Norwich; he quickly rose to foreman and then to general foreman, and by 1921 he was married and running his own business.

From the outset, the whole family was involved in the venture; his uncles helped him financially, his wife Florence acted as secretary, bookkeeper and wages clerk and her brother Ted drove the horse and trolley, and later the motor lorry. George worked tirelessly to get his business up and running, but always managed to find time for his children, Robert Edward, Betty, Mary and Ruth. Where work was concerned, his guiding rule was that a contract had to be completed on time even if it meant working from six in the morning until ten in the evening during the summer months. When a contract was finished he liked to put up hoardings emblazoned with the firm's proud boast, On Time Again!. He would not tolerate timewasters, but he would reward hard work, and this created great loyalty among his workforce.

Having survived the depression of the late 1920s and early 1930s, George decided in 1932 to turn the firm into a limited company. His son Bob joined R G Carter Limited as an apprentice carpenter six years later, but unfortunately his early career was interrupted, as his father's had been, by the outbreak of war. The firm obtained a steady stream of Government contracts; one of the more unusual jobs the construction of a fake city, complete with homes and factories, at Withernsea, as a decoy to draw German bombers away from nearby Hull.

Above: *Long Causeway Chambers, adjacent to Queensway Shopping Centre.* ***Below:*** *The administrative Centre of the Norwich and Peterborough Building Society at the Lynch Wood Business Park.*

Bob Carter returned in 1946, and took over as managing director in 1950. In the early 50s, under Bob Carter's leadership, business began to boom, and by the mid-1950s, R G Carter had become the largest building firm in Norfolk.

R.G. Carter's presence in Peterborough arose out of its King's Lynn company. It was a move initiated in the late 60s to meet demand by the Peterborough Development Corporation for commercial space and residential properties. In 1985 the company also built Stuart House in the heart of the city, at 11, 500 square metres the largest office block to be commissioned by the Corporation.

Among other landmark constructions are the Norwich and Peterborough Building Society administrative centre at Lynch Wood; the regional office for the National Rivers Authority; the Magistrates' Courts; and, outside the city, the officers' air crew selection centre at RAF Cranwell.

R.G. Carter opened its first office in Peterborough in 1983 at 5 Cowgate largely to control the development of Stuart House.

The years following saw many interesting contracts. Among them were the Granary Beefeater Steak House at Orton Meadows; the complete refurbishment of Long Causeway Chambers to create modern shop units and offices adjacent to the Queensgate shopping centre; the Bretton Baptist Church at the Copelands Centre; the Werrington local shopping and community centre; and National Westminster's pavilion at the East of England Showground.

Not surprisingly the company rapidly outgrew its offices, moving in 1986 to its present site at Padholme Road East, Peterborough. (Telephone: 01733 312881).

The Group is currently enjoying the most successful period in its history under the chairmanship of Robert Carter, Bob's son. This family tradition, now in its third generation, is a crucial element in the stability and security of the workforce and the continued expansion and success of the company.

Top left: *The Peterborough British Rail Electrification Fixed Equipment Maintenance Distribution Depot.* ***Below:*** *RG Carter's purpose built offices and builder's yard at Padholme Road East.* ***Bottom:*** *Part of the Stuart House city-centre office block at Peterborough.*

Solutions for your financial affairs

Stephenson, Smart & Co., the chartered accountants of Church Walk, were started by Mr Smart in 1882. Peterborough then was still a country town where livestock were marketed on the unpaved streets and professional men of affairs, such as Mr Smart, catered for local landowners and the allied businesses of the rural hinterland. Like most towns of the period Peterborough had its own breweries and seed and corn merchants, which together with the harness and saddlery trade essential to a horse drawn economy provided much of his custom.

The two railway stations of the Great Northern Railway eased the transport of agrarian and industrial goods between producers and consumers in the days when railway companies and trade expanded together. The major hotels such as The Bull and The Grand, added to the railway's own hotel, catering as they were for the new breed of commercial travellers as well as the local gentry and farmers visiting town for business and social events, were large enough to employ an accountant to oversee their books.

Professional men of the period practiced in their own homes, often furnished to impress their clients, located either in the town centre or in the new, leafy suburban streets of spacious late Victorian villas. In 1904 Joseph Stephenson provided new blood and ideas for the practice of Mr Smart who died in 1912 leaving Mr Stephenson to develop the business. As the market town changed its character and grew towards its present position as the industrial and service industry centre of its region so too grew the firm of Stephenson Smart.

By 1924 it had moved into premises in Queen Street, in which impressive

***Top right:** Joseph Stephenson escorting the Duke and Duchess of Gloucester at the Peterborough Show just after the war.*
***Left:** The Queen Street Chambers.*

surroundings the company gathered strength and built up a reputation second to none. The Joseph Stephenson practice expanded during the 1930s from what became the Head Office in Peterborough with branch offices in London, Liverpool and York and 33 other places. A considerable achievement in the days when most professional men were content to be big fish in local pools.

After service during the second world war Major Leonard Stephenson joined his father's practice in which Alfred Sutcliffe and Reginald Sutcliffe were partners. Two of the present partners were admitted into the partnership in the late sixties. By the early nineties the practice outgrew its Queen Street premises and in 1994 moved to purpose built offices in Church Walk. Today this is an accountancy practice which continues to lead the way in offering its clients expertise in the most up-to-date methods available. As taxation legislation, and the means to reduce its impact, become yearly more complex, the need for greater specialist knowledge increases. Some accountancy firms increase their staff or amalgamate with others to acquire this knowledge often at a loss of the personal attention which is vital to the individual client.

Stephenson Smart avoid the pitfalls and yet have access to the wider expertise by their membership of The UK 200 Group, a national association of independent accountants of similar size dedicated to providing the best service to their clients. Additionally Stephenson Smart continue to liaise on good terms with the Inland Revenue, the VAT experts of HM Customs and Excise, and all banks, solicitors and other accountants in the locality.

One thing which does not change is the firm's insistence on courtesy and personal service. The staff find that clients, great and small, relate more comfortably when treated as individuals whose business is worthy of their time and skills. This is achieved by linking each client to a single member of the team who always looks after that client's interests and so builds up knowledge and understanding of each person's or company's business. Only then can the 'Crichton' like interpretation of tax laws be tailored to the needs of each customer for their ultimate benefit.

Private individuals wishing to safeguard their family's interests will find Stephenson Smart can advise them in their planning for the future as well as assist them in easing day to day monetary problems. Those starting, running or expanding any business can draw upon the firm's experience in dealing with legal aspects, business plans, audits and budgeting while payroll services are equally available to small charities and large firms alike.

Top left: *The partners and managers pictured when the new office opened in 1994.*
Below: *The firm's present offices at 15 Church Walk, Peterborough.*

Cooking up new inventions

The APV Baker group of companies is responsible for the manufacture of a varied range of modern machinery. Thanks to their innovations and developments bread, biscuit, cereal and confectionery making is easier and more efficient. APV Baker, formerly Baker Perkins, is an organisation which thrives on innovation, remaining true to the traditions of the two families which joined forces in 1920 to form Joseph Baker Sons & Perkins Limited.

The Baker family business had begun with the invention of a single ingenious device - a flour scoop and sifter combined, patented in 1870 by Joseph Baker of Maple Ridge, near Trenton, Ontario, Canada. The family then set up a London factory which manufactured patent food machinery, such as the Revolving or Reel Oven for biscuit-making and a machine for making sugar wafers. By the time of its incorporation in 1902 the company had some 350 employees and was

exporting a significant proportion of its output. The following decade Joseph Baker & Sons found itself in dispute with a rival, Werner, Pfleiderer & Perkins, over an alleged patent infringement concerning its automatic bread plant.The dispute led to tentative plans to amalgamate, and two concerns finally united after the first world war.

The founder of A M Perkins & Son was an even more prolific inventor than was the founder of the Baker business. Jacob Perkins, born 1766, invented nail machines, pumps for fire-engines, coining machines, ship ventilation, a safety lock for bank vaults, stereotype steel plates for printing bank notes, and the Perkins printing process which produced the Penny Black, he also worked on a process of mechanical refrigeration, and perhaps his most famous achievement of all was the Perkins steam engine. Unfortunately he was never able to convert his remarkable inventions into commercial successes. The firm went on to make further engineering breakthroughs such as the Perkins patent oven, all of them excellent products which somehow failed to bring the firm the financial rewards it deserved, and it was not until its takeover by Joseph Baker that financial security was finally assured.

Since that time APV Baker has gone on to bring us many new machines, too many to list; suffice it to say that all over the world everyday tasks are made easier and the quality of life is enhanced by Baker Perkins machinery.

Top left: *Company Founder, Joseph Baker.* ***Left:*** *A special frozen food version of the Rose Forgrove 'Transwrap' 7D at the Cleethorpes factory of Findus Eskimo Food Ltd.* ***Top right:*** *A line of Rose Forgrove RTC machines, supplied by Baker Perkins Ltd, cartoning sponge cakes at Lyons Bakery, Wakefield.*

Nene Housing - second to none

Throughout its history Nene Housing Society has worked to provide both new and refurbished homes for its tenants. The ideal of enabling them to enjoy attractive, well equipped homes in pleasant surroundings is paramount.

Nene was formed in 1973 by concerned housing experts to fill this need in the Peterborough, Nottingham and Northampton areas. Within two years there were over a thousand homes available

or being made ready for tenants at rents of from £6.25 a week.

The Society continued to expand rapidly and opened its second management office in Nottingham in 1977. Government funding cutbacks in the 1980s curtailed growth but by 1983 Nene had 1,500 homes completed bringing in rental income of £1m a year. During this period many homeless people and applicants from council's waiting lists were provided with good quality homes.

Having to cope with less government funds did not deter Nene. Money was raised from private sources to provide more homes for rent and for many affordable home ownership schemes. Help with special housing projects was given by Nene to many small charities.

Nene is now a registered charity and is the largest locally based housing association in the Peterborough area with a turnover of £6m and a staff of 90. Much of the Society's work is now carried out in partnership with councils and other agencies making sure that new social housing is in the right location and built to high standards. Improvement work to Nene's housing, first built in the 1970s, features as a high priority together with some specific projects for disabled people and the elderly.

The first 25 years has been a remarkable success story, long may it continue.

Top: *Nene's first sheltered housing complex, Sudbury Court.* ***Left:*** *Westhay Court, Nottingham.* ***Below:*** *The Founder Members.*

Sugar from the roots

Sugar was hardly known in Europe before the 15th century when cane sugar was first imported from the West Indies. This initially expensive luxury quickly replaced honey as a sweetener of food and drinks, not least in 18th century beer, thanks to pressure by powerful West Indies planters. Although many people find it difficult to equate the muddy roots of sugar beet as a source of sugar this has been the case since 1748 when a Prussian scientist succeeded in obtaining sugar from beet plants.

Napoleon encouraged French farmers to overcome the Royal Navy's blockade by growing beet sugar. By 1900 sugar beet was an important crop throughout mainland Europe but not in Britain. In 1909 the National Sugar Beet Association was set up to encourage the growth of a crop unfamiliar to British farmers and to foster processing into sugar. Early efforts were unprofitable although in other countries 45percent of the world's sugar output came from beet grown in temperate climates while the greater proportion came from tropical sugar cane plantations.

The outbreak of war in 1914 cut Britain off from both West Indian cane sugar and from European beet sugar. The British Sugar Beet Society was founded to fill the gap both during and after the Great War. The pre-war factory at Cantley in Norfolk was supplemented by other independent factories until there were 18.

The huge processing plants need vast quantities of water to clean, transport and process the beet roots as they are processed into black treacle, golden syrup and various grades of sugar. The plant material is dried into shreds and sold to livestock farmers as sugar beet pulp, a tasty supplement to the winter rations of beasts kept indoors or in yards.

Top: *Dried molassed sugar beet, a popular form of animal feed.* ***Left:*** *A farmer inspects his crop of sugar beet.* ***Below:*** *Until the late 1940s, sugar was stored and transported in 3cwt jute or 1cwt paper sacks.*

The state of the industry between the wars was so precarious that it almost collapsed in the face of cheap foreign supplies and government disinterest until the formation of the British Sugar Corporation in 1936 amalgamated all the independent factories. Ten years later Britain, once again at war, struggled to feed herself from her own sadly neglected farms. The Ministry of Food took dictatorial steps to encourage the rebirth of farming and to provide the most useful crops for a strictly rationed population. Sugar was rationed to half a pound a week and sweets to 4 ounces a week per person until 1953. Post war advertisements for Mars Bars showed them cut into seven portions, one for each day of the week!

The production of sugar from 395,000 acres had so worn the factories' plant that by 1945 this was in urgent need of replacement. Although the government held some 36percent of shares until 1981 the BSC was an independent body which financed a programme of modernisation between 1950 and 1955. Following which the commercially successful BSC has continued to upgrade it factories and the marketing of its products under the popular Silver Spoon label, which replaced the original trade mark in 1972.

During the 1960/61 campaign the re-equipped factories handled an astonishing 7,200,000 tons of beet from which 900,000 tons of sugar were won. Modernisation had reduced labour requirements by 50percent. During this decade old hand harvesting methods gave way to mechanical sugar beet harvesters which trawled through the flat fields of Eastern England. Storage in sealed silos became common and the food processing and drinks industries became major customers for liquid sugar.

Threats, in 1979, by the European Community to cut British Sugar production by 30percent treble the cuts in Europe, were fought off as the government changed from Labour to Conservative. These cuts would have cost nearly half the jobs in BSC, the closure of eight out of seventeen factories and hammered British farmers by the loss of 250,000 acres of sugar beet. Next year beet farmers planted 520,000 acres to ensure that Britons ate British sugar.

The company was purchased by Associated British Foods in 1991 and continuous investment has resulted in a leaner fitter environmentally conscious company operating from nine factories. Two of these have their immediate surroundings designated as Sites of Special Scientific Interest while the valuable water used in processing is returned well cleaned to rivers. The current well trained workforce is taking a confident company into the future.

Top: *Raw sugar being stored in the warehouse prior to white sugar production and silos, 1950s.*
Below: *Peterborough factory staff gather for a group photograph in 1996.*

From rags to riches

When Mr Thomas and Mr Green established their paper mill in 1705 they were following a trade dating back to the Ancient Egyptians and the Chinese, the latter being the first to use paper money. English paper makers of the 18th Century used shredded rags as the raw material, a substance still used in the most expensive stationery today. It was then usual for paper makers to be located near water for power and within easy reach of large towns from which the rags were obtained.

One of the occupational hazards of the time were the outbreaks of smallpox brought to the mill by the contaminated clothing from jails, such hospitals as existed and the growing chain of workhouses. When the Bucks County Roll was taken in 1798, a year when the desperately over stretched army was somewhat aided by Militia Volunteers being sent to Ireland, 166 paper workers were concentrated in a

Right: *Arborfield Mill, formerly home to Towgood & Beckwith before Thomas & Green Ltd took over the site.*
Below: *Paper Machine, circa 1908.*

mere five parishes. Having survived punitive wartime taxation the growing paper factory, in 1830, had its new machines broken by latter-day Luddites fearing their job security, they were transported to Botany Bay and van Diemen's Land.

The company has survived these unpleasantly troubled industrial relations and the equally revolutionary introduction of electricity!

Thomas & Green moved from Buckinghamshire to Helpston, outside Peterborough, some twenty years ago. It is an ideal location with good road connections between the East Coast ports and the industrial Midlands while changes in the rural infrastructure enable the firm to draw upon local labour.

In 1979 Thomas & Green bought Arborfield Mill, formerly the site of Towgood & Beckwith's paper company. The Helpston site was first opened in 1856, originally as the Lincolnshire Twitch Paper & Millboard Company Limited; set up to manufacture paper out of the local couch grass. When this project failed the mill lay empty until 1861, when it was taken over by the Towgood family after a fire had destroyed their mill at Arborfield, near Reading; hence they named the mill at Helpston 'Arborfield', and used it to produce wrapping papers for their two other mills.

Over the years Thomas & Green Ltd has pioneered many of the processes used throughout the papermaking industry and manufactured a huge range of quality paper goods. Today they specialise in the production of high quality coffee filter papers for both the catering and household markets and their products are used by some of the most famous names in the coffee industry throughout the world - exporting 80 percent of their total production to 27 countries.

Many people will remember the days when milk was filtered through paper filters on the farm and sand, sugar and chemicals were separated in school laboratory experiments using paper filters. The highly sophisticated papers used in Thomas & Green filters are produced at the associated GT Mandl Group mill in Switzerland, a country where quality always wins the fight with accountants. As a member of this international group Thomas & Green enjoys advantages in price and marketing. The company is pleased to be one of the first paper makers to have achieved BS/EN/ISO 9002 recognition.

Top left: *Thomas & Green's current premises.*
Below: *An aerial view of Thomas & Green.*

Perkin's 21st birthday celebrations on 4th September 1953 were marked, amongst other events, with swings, roundabouts and rides for the children of their employees.

Perkins' Sports and Family Day in June 1957.

Acknowledgments

Local Studies Collection - Peterborough Central Library

Perkins Engines Company Limited

Richard Hillier

Stephen Perry

Thanks are also due to

Peggy Burns who penned the editorial text

and Margaret Wakefield and Mike Kirke for their copywriting skills